Bible Promises

to Treasure

for Couples

Bible Promises
to Treasure
for Couples

Inspiring

words

for every

occasion

Nashville, Tennessee

Bible Promises to Treasure for Couples
© 1998 Broadman & Holman Publishers,
Nashville, Tennessee
All rights reserved
Printed in Belgium

ISBN# 1–55819–713–3

Dewey Decimal Classification: 306.87
Subject Heading: MARRIAGE
Library of Congress Card Catalog Number: 97–25917

******

A note on the sources of quotations. When possible I have supplied at least the book name from which contemporary quotes have come. Yet even this is often impossible, since many came from my "journal of jottings" over many years. Also, if a quote is from a person who lived longer than fifty or so years ago, I've made no attempt to cite the source. Such quotations are usually available in any standard book of quotes.

******

All Scripture passages are from the Authorized King James Version.

Library of Congress Cataloging-in-Publication Data
Bible promises to treasure for couples / compiled by Gary Wilde.
   p. cm.
   Includes bibliographical references.
   ISBN 1–55819–713–3 (hc)
      1. Spouses—Religious life—Quotations. 2. Marriage—Religious aspects—Christianity—Quotations, maxims, etc.
   I. Wilde, Gary.
BV4596.M3P76   1998
248.8'44—dc21

97–25917
CIP

1 2 3 4 5 6   02 01 00 99 98

Contents

Introduction

—One—

Strengthening Your Commitment   5

—Two—

Keeping the Communication Lines Open   25

v

Introduction

I remember as a child singing often at church: "Standing on the Promises of God." Or maybe it was mostly the adults who were singing; but I was standing next to them—my parents and all the others. I recall those faithful people joyfully reciting words they must surely have known by heart . . .

**When the howling storms
of doubt and fear assail,
By the living Word of God I shall prevail,
Standing on the promises of God.**

For years Downey Church, in sunny central Florida, had preached and taught the promises

1

of God and believed in His goodness. From the beginning—when the church building was a small tin-roofed, A-frame at the east end of a dirt road on the outskirts of Orlando—people would gather to stand on the immutable promises. Under the shiny tin roof, standing on the sandy-wooden floorboards, they melded their voices to the tunes of the upright piano and recalled God's goodness. Today, as the church there grows and thrives—now there is also a school and gymnasium—I can only attribute its vibrant life to a love of God's promises and the recognition that without the pledges that flow from the mouth of God, there is no church, no music, and no reason for either.

The promises of God have always been the bedrock of Christian faith; for without God's sacred covenants with us, we cannot survive. In times of joy or heartache, in all our ups and downs, we keep coming back to that source of our life: the motivation for all our doing and the reason for our existence. It is the message of God's mighty assurances: this life is not all there is, He will always be with us while we are here, and He will take us to be with Him someday.

Yes, we do have priceless promises to keep close to our hearts!

My hope for you as you delve into this scriptural treasure chest is that you will grow deeper in love with the One who has spoken as no other ever could. With so many influences bombarding our minds each moment of the day, what could be better than to set aside a few moments of quiet to hear the still, small voice that constantly invites us into warm fellowship? We'll be richly rewarded if we truly listen to what that voice is saying. His words convey blessing and guidance, wisdom and warning, life for now and life everlasting. What incomparable grace!

Gary Wilde
Colorado Springs, 1997

One

Strengthening Your Commitment

What a wonderful thing to be in relationship! The affection and intimacy we can know was God's idea from the beginning, for it mirrors His own nature—the three-in-one of the Godhead eternally loving and relating. Naturally, then, His Word offers great encouragement for us. It calls us to strengthen the bonds of our commitments to one another, and to Him.

5

Remember the Spiritual Significance of Your Relationship

A good marriage is not a contract between two persons but a sacred covenant between three. Too often Christ is never invited to the wedding and finds no room in the home. Why? Is it because we have misrepresented Him and forgotten His joyful outlook on life?

—*Donald T. Kauffman[1]*

The LORD God said, It is not good that the man should be alone; I will make him an help meet for him.

And out of the ground the LORD God formed every beast of the field, and every fowl of the air; and brought them unto Adam to see what he would call them: and whatsoever Adam called every living creature, that was the name thereof.

And Adam gave names to all cattle, and to the fowl of the air, and to every beast of the field; but for Adam there was not found an help meet for him.

And the LORD God caused a deep sleep to fall upon Adam and he slept: and he took one of his ribs, and closed up the flesh instead thereof;

And the rib, which the LORD God had taken from man, made he a woman, and brought her unto the man.

And Adam said, This is now bone of my bones, and flesh of my flesh: she shall be called Woman, because she was taken out of Man.

Therefore shall a man leave his father and his mother, and shall cleave unto his wife: and they shall be one flesh.

And they were both naked, the man and his wife, and were not ashamed.

—*Genesis 2:18–25*

For thy Maker is thine husband; the LORD of hosts is his name; and thy Redeemer the Holy One of Israel; The God of the whole earth shall he be called.

—*Isaiah 54:5*

7

Turn, O backsliding children, saith the LORD; for I am married unto you: and I will take you one of a city, and two of a family, and I will bring you to Zion.

—Jeremiah 3:14

Marriage is honourable in all, and the bed undefiled.

—Hebrews 13:4a

When a man hath taken a new wife, he shall not go out to war, neither shall he be charged with any business: but he shall be free at home one year, and shall cheer up his wife which he hath taken.

—Deuteronomy 24:5

Adore Your Mate!

When I walk on the beach to watch the sunset I do not call out, "A little more orange over to the right, please," or "Would you mind giving us less purple in the back?"
No, I enjoy the always-different sunsets as they are. We do well to do the same with people we love."

—Carl Rogers

My beloved is white and ruddy, the chiefest among ten thousand.

His head is as the most fine gold, his locks are bushy, and black as a raven.

His eyes are as the eyes of doves by the rivers of waters, washed with milk, and fitly set.

His cheeks are as a bed of spices, as sweet flowers: his lips like lilies, dropping sweet smelling myrrh.

His hands are as gold rings set with the beryl: his belly is as bright ivory overlaid with sapphires.

His legs are as pillars of marble, set upon sockets of fine gold: his countenance is as Lebanon, excellent as the cedars.

His mouth is most sweet: yea, he is altogether lovely. This is my beloved, and this is my friend, O daughters of Jerusalem.

—Song of Solomon 5:10–16

Stay Faithful to One Another

Marriages may be made in heaven, but people are responsible for the maintenance work.
—*Anonymous*

Let thy fountain be blessed: and rejoice with the wife of thy youth.

Let her be as the loving hind and pleasant roe; let her breasts satisfy thee at all times; and be thou ravished always with her love.

And why wilt thou, my son, be ravished with a strange woman, and embrace the bosom of a stranger?

—*Proverbs 5:18–20*

When wisdom entereth into thine heart, and knowledge is pleasant unto thy soul;

Discretion shall preserve thee, understanding shall keep thee:

To deliver thee from the way of the evil man, from the man that speaketh froward things;

Who leave the paths of uprightness, to walk in the ways of darkness;

Who rejoice to do evil, and delight in the frowardness of the wicked;

Whose ways are crooked, and they froward in their paths:

To deliver thee from the strange woman, even from the stranger which flattereth with her words;

Which forsaketh the guide of her youth, and forgetteth the covenant of her God.

For her house inclineth unto death, and her paths unto the dead.

None that go unto her return again, neither take they hold of the paths of life.

That thou mayest walk in the way of good men, and keep the paths of the righteous.

—Proverb 2:10–20

Ye have heard that it was said by them of old time, Thou shalt not commit adultery:

But I say unto you, That whosoever looketh on a woman to lust after her hath committed adultery with her already in his heart.

—Matthew 5:27–28

Meats for the belly, and the belly for meats: but God shall destroy both it and them. Now the body is not for fornication, but for the Lord; and the Lord for the body.

And God hath both raised up the Lord, and will also raise up us by his own power.

Know ye not that your bodies are the members of Christ? shall I then take the members of Christ, and make them the members of an harlot? God forbid.

—1 Corinthians 6:13–15

There hath no temptation taken you but such as is common to man: but God is faithful, who will not suffer you to be tempted above that ye are able; but will with the temptation also make a way to escape, that ye may be able to bear it.

—1 Corinthians 10:13

Flee also youthful lusts: but follow righteousness, faith, charity, peace, with them that call on the Lord out of a pure heart.

—2 Timothy 2:22

Dearly beloved, I beseech you as strangers and pilgrims, abstain from fleshly lusts, which war against the soul.

—1 Peter 2:11

12

Develop Staying-Power in Your Relationship

What I call a good patient is one who, having found a good physician, sticks to him till he dies.

—*Oliver Wendell Holmes*

Although the fig tree shall not blossom, neither shall fruit be in the vines; the labour of the olive shall fail, and the fields shall yield no meat; the flock shall be cut off from the fold, and there shall be no herd in the stalls:

Yet I will rejoice in the LORD, I will joy in the God of my salvation.

The LORD God is my strength, and he will make my feet like hinds' feet, and he will make me to walk upon mine high places. To the chief singer on my stringed instruments.

—*Habakkuk 3:17–19*

For the which cause I also suffer these things: nevertheless I am not ashamed: for I know whom I have believed, and am

13

persuaded that he is able to keep that which I have committed unto him against that day.

—2 Timothy 1:12

This know also, that in the last days perilous times shall come.

For men shall be lovers of their own selves, covetous, boasters, proud, blasphemers, disobedient to parents, unthankful, unholy,

Without natural affection, trucebreakers, false accusers, incontinent, fierce, despisers of those that are good,

Traitors, heady, highminded, lovers of pleasures more than lovers of God.

—2 Timothy 3:1–4

Defer to One Another in Humility

To keep your marriage brimming
With love in the loving cup,
If ever you're wrong, admit it,
If ever you're right, shut up.

—Ogden Nash

Submitting yourselves one to another in the fear of God.

—*Ephesians 5:21*

Likewise, ye husbands, dwell with them according to knowledge, giving honour unto the wife, as unto the weaker vessel, and as being heirs together of the grace of life; that your prayers be not hindered.

—*1 Peter 3:7*

Husbands, love your wives, even as Christ also loved the church, and gave himself for it;

That he might sanctify and cleanse it with the washing of water by the word,

That he might present it to himself a glorious church, not having spot, or wrinkle, or any such thing; but that it should be holy and without blemish.

So ought men to love their wives as their own bodies. He that loveth his wife loveth himself.

For no man ever yet hated his own flesh; but nourisheth and cherisheth it, even as the Lord the church:

For we are members of his body, of his flesh, and of his bones.

For this cause shall a man leave his father and mother, and shall be joined unto his wife, and they two shall be one flesh.

This is a great mystery: but I speak concerning Christ and the church.

Nevertheless let every one of you in particular so love his wife even as himself; and the wife see that she reverence her husband.

—*Ephesians 5:25–33*

Strive to Be Helpful and Thoughtful Toward One Another

I saw a story about a woman who was away for a few days at a teachers' convention. Suddenly she remembered it was Monday, trash day, and she expressed her concern to her friend. But her friend tried to calm her fears, reminding her that her husband was still at home and he could certainly put out the trash by himself. But she said, "It takes both of us to take out the trash. I can't carry it and he can't remember it."

—*James Hewett[2]*

16

Bear ye one another's burdens, and so fulfil the law of Christ.

For if a man think himself to be something, when he is nothing, he deceiveth himself.

But let every man prove his own work, and then shall he have rejoicing in himself alone, and not in another.

—*Galatians 6:2–4*

With all lowliness and meekness, with longsuffering, forbearing one another in love;

Endeavouring to keep the unity of the Spirit in the bond of peace.

—*Ephesians 4:2–3*

Then Jesus six days before the passover came to Bethany, where Lazarus was which had been dead, whom he raised from the dead.

There they made him a supper; and Martha served: but Lazarus was one of them that sat at the table with him.

Then took Mary a pound of ointment of spikenard, very costly, and anointed the feet of Jesus, and wiped his feet with her hair: and the house was filled with the odour of the ointment.

17

Then saith one of his disciples, Judas Iscariot, Simon's son, which should betray him,

Why was not this ointment sold for three hundred pence, and given to the poor?

This he said, not that he cared for the poor; but because he was a thief, and had the bag, and bare what was put therein.

Then said Jesus, Let her alone: against the day of my burying hath she kept this.

—*John 12:1–7*

Don't Follow in the Path of These Couples!

A mighty tree stood high upon the mountain. It survived the hail, the heavy snows, the storms, the bitter cold of many years. Then finally it was felled by an attack of the little beetles. And so it is with marriage.

—*James Hewett*[3]

❤ *Herod and Herodias*

And king Herod heard of him; (for his name was spread abroad:) and he said, That John the Baptist was risen from the dead, and

18

therefore mighty works do shew forth themselves in him.

Others said, That it is Elias. And others said, That it is a prophet, or as one of the prophets.

But when Herod heard thereof, he said, It is John, whom I beheaded: he is risen from the dead.

For Herod himself had sent forth and laid hold upon John, and bound him in prison for Herodias' sake, his brother Philip's wife: for he had married her.

For John had said unto Herod, It is not lawful for thee to have thy brother's wife.

Therefore Herodias had a quarrel against him, and would have killed him; but she could not:

For Herod feared John, knowing that he was a just man and an holy, and observed him; and when he heard him, he did many things, and heard him gladly.

—Mark 6:14–20

❤ *Samson and Delilah*

It came to pass afterward, that [Samson] loved a woman in the valley of Sorek, whose name was Delilah.

And the lords of the Philistines came up unto her, and said unto her, Entice him, and see wherein his great strength lieth, and by what means we may prevail against him, that we may bind him to afflict him: and we will give thee every one of us eleven hundred pieces of silver.

And Delilah said to Samson, Tell me, I pray thee, wherein thy great strength lieth, and wherewith thou mightest be bound to afflict thee.

And Samson said unto her, If they bind me with seven green withs that were never dried, then shall I be weak, and be as another man.

Then the lords of the Philistines brought up to her seven green withs which had not been dried, and she bound him with them.

Now there were men lying in wait, abiding with her in the chamber. And she said unto him, The Philistines be upon thee, Samson. And he brake the withs, as a thread of tow is broken when it toucheth the fire. So his strength was not known.

And Delilah said unto Samson, Behold, thou hast mocked me, and told me lies: now tell me, I pray thee, wherewith thou mightest be bound.

And he said unto her, If they bind me fast with new ropes that never were occupied, then shall I be weak, and be as another man.

Delilah therefore took new ropes, and bound him therewith, and said unto him, The Philistines be upon thee, Samson. And there were liers in wait abiding in the chamber. And he brake them from off his arms like a thread.

And Delilah said unto Samson, Hitherto thou hast mocked me, and told me lies: tell me wherewith thou mightest be bound. And he said unto her, If thou weavest the seven locks of my head with the web.

And she fastened it with the pin, and said unto him, The Philistines be upon thee, Samson. And he awaked out of his sleep, and went away with the pin of the beam, and with the web.

And she said unto him, How canst thou say, I love thee, when thine heart is not with me? thou hast mocked me these three times, and hast not told me wherein thy great strength lieth.

And it came to pass, when she pressed him daily with her words, and urged him, so that his soul was vexed unto death.

—Judges 16:4–16

❤ *Ahab and Jezebel*

In the thirty and eighth year of Asa king of Judah began Ahab the son of Omri to reign over Israel: and Ahab the son of Omri reigned over Israel in Samaria twenty and two years.

And Ahab the son of Omri did evil in the sight of the LORD above all that were before him.

And it came to pass, as if it had been a light thing for him to walk in the sins of Jeroboam the son of Nebat, that he took to wife Jezebel the daughter of Ethbaal king of the Zidonians, and went and served Baal, and worshipped him.

And he reared up an altar for Baal in the house of Baal, which he had built in Samaria.

And Ahab made a grove; and Ahab did more to provoke the LORD God of Israel to anger than all the kings of Israel that were before him.

In his days did Hiel the Bethelite build Jericho: he laid the foundation thereof in Abiram his first-born, and set up the gates thereof in his youngest son Segub, according to the word of the LORD, which he spake by Joshua the son of Nun.

—*1 Kings 16:29–34*

Avoid the Heartache of Divorce

Marriage used to be a contract. Now many regard it as a ninety-day option.

—*Anonymous*

The Pharisees also came unto him, tempting him, and saying unto him, Is it lawful for a man to put away his wife for every cause?

And he answered and said unto them, Have ye not read, that he which made them at the beginning made them male and female,

And said, For this cause shall a man leave father and mother, and shall cleave to his wife: and they twain shall be one flesh?

23

Wherefore they are no more twain, but one flesh. What therefore God hath joined together, let not man put asunder.

They say unto him, Why did Moses then command to give a writing of divorcement, and to put her away?

He saith unto them, Moses because of the hardness of your hearts suffered you to put away your wives: but from the beginning it was not so.

And I say unto you, Whosoever shall put away his wife, except it be for fornication, and shall marry another, committeth adultery: and whoso marrieth her which is put away doth commit adultery.

—*Matthew 19:3–9*

— T w o —

Keeping the Communication Lines Open

When it comes to growing a relationship, communication is the key. Sadly, we can relate for years on a purely superficial level, never revealing what it is that "makes us tick"—our joys and sorrows, our hopes and fears.

When we become courageous enough to bring our whole selves before God, we are surprised to discover that He chooses to love every part we have offered Him. That is the goal for couples, too. We can only love what we know of one another.

25

Really Listen to One Another!

Somewhere we know that without silence words lose their meaning, that without listening speaking no longer heals, that without distance closeness cannot cure.

—Henri Nouwen

The heart of the prudent getteth knowledge; and the ear of the wise seeketh knowledge.

—*Proverbs 18:15*

Wherefore, Job, I pray thee, hear my speeches, and hearken to all my words.

Behold, now I have opened my mouth, my tongue hath spoken in my mouth.

My words shall be of the uprightness of my heart: and my lips shall utter knowledge clearly.

The spirit of God hath made me, and the breath of the Almighty hath given me life.

If thou canst answer me, set thy words in order before me, stand up.

—*Job 33:1–5*

Then Samuel said unto Saul, Stay, and I will tell thee what the LORD hath said to me this night. And he said unto him, Say on.

—*1 Samuel 15:16*

A man hath joy by the answer of his mouth: and a word spoken in due season, how good is it!

—*Proverbs 15:23*

Speak Lovingly and Honestly

The genius of communication is the ability to be both totally honest and totally kind at the same time.

—*John Powell*[1]

But speaking the truth in love, may [you] grow up into him in all things, which is the head, even Christ:

From whom the whole body fitly joined together and compacted by that which every joint supplieth, according to the effectual working in the measure of every part, maketh increase of the body unto the edifying of itself in love.

—*Ephesians 4:15–16*

27

Speaking to yourselves in psalms and hymns and spiritual songs, singing and making melody in your heart to the Lord;

Giving thanks always for all things unto God and the Father in the name of our Lord Jesus Christ.

—Ephesians 5:19–20

We were gentle among you, even as a nurse cherisheth her children.

—1 Thessalonians 2:7

Who shall ascend into the hill of the LORD? or who shall stand in his holy place?

He that hath clean hands, and a pure heart; who hath not lifted up his soul unto vanity, nor sworn deceitfully.

—Psalm 24:3–4

Share with Your Mate When You're Feeling 'Down'

Never awake me when you have good news to announce, because with good news nothing presses; but when you have bad news, arouse me immediately, for then there is not an instant to be lost.

—*Napoleon I*

And it shall be, when they say unto thee, Wherefore sighest thou? that thou shalt answer, For the tidings; because it cometh: and every heart shall melt, and all hands shall be feeble, and every spirit shall faint, and all knees shall be weak as water.

—*Ezekiel 21:7a*

When I would comfort myself against sorrow, my heart is faint in me.

—*Jeremiah 8:18*

Come unto me, all ye that labour and are heavy laden, and I will give you rest.

Take my yoke upon you, and learn of me; for I am meek and lowly in heart: and ye shall find rest unto your souls.

For my yoke is easy, and my burden is light.

—*Matthew 11:28–30*

For this thing I besought the Lord thrice, that it might depart from me.

And he said unto me, My grace is sufficient for thee: for my strength is made perfect in weakness. Most gladly therefore will I rather glory in my infirmities, that the power of Christ may rest upon me. . . .

For though he was crucified through weakness, yet he liveth by the power of God. For we also are weak in him, but we shall live with him by the power of God toward you.

—*2 Corinthians 12:8–9; 13:4*

Finally, my brethren, be strong in the Lord, and in the power of his might.

—*Ephesians 6:10*

Prove Yourself Trustworthy in Everything

Duty does not have to be dull. Love can make it beautiful and fill it with life.

—*Thomas Merton*

Take ye heed every one of his neighbour, and trust ye not in any brother: for every brother will utterly supplant, and every neighbour will walk with slanders.

—*Jeremiah 9:4*

And God blessed them, and God said unto them, Be fruitful, and multiply, and replenish the earth, and subdue it: and have dominion over the fish of the sea, and over the fowl of the air, and over every living thing that moveth upon the earth.

And God said, Behold, I have given you every herb bearing seed, which is upon the face of all the earth, and every tree, in the which is the fruit of a tree yielding seed; to you it shall be for meat.

And to every beast of the earth, and to every fowl of the air, and to every thing that creepeth upon the earth, wherein there is life, I have given every green herb for meat: and it was so.

—*Genesis 1:28–30*

Yet they tempted and provoked the most high God, and kept not his testimonies:

But turned back, and dealt unfaithfully like their fathers: they were turned aside like a deceitful bow.

For they provoked him to anger with their high places, and moved him to jealousy with their graven images.

When God heard this, he was wroth, and greatly abhorred Israel:

So that he forsook the tabernacle of Shiloh, the tent which he placed among men;

And delivered his strength into captivity, and his glory into the enemy's hand.

He gave his people over also unto the sword; and was wroth with his inheritance.

The fire consumed their young men; and their maidens were not given to marriage.

Their priests fell by the sword; and their widows made no lamentation.

—*Psalm 78:56–64*

A talebearer revealeth secrets: but he that is of a faithful spirit concealeth the matter.

—*Proverbs 11:13*

Therefore, brethren, we are debtors, not to the flesh, to live after the flesh.

For if ye live after the flesh, ye shall die: but if ye through the Spirit do mortify the deeds of the body, ye shall live.

—*Romans 8:12–13*

And they that are Christ's have crucified the flesh with the affections and lusts.

—*Galatians 5:24*

For the grace of God that bringeth salvation hath appeared to all men,

Teaching us that, denying ungodliness and worldly lusts, we should live soberly, righteously, and godly, in this present world;

—*Titus 2:11–12*

Maintain a Spirit of Togetherness and Teamwork

Marriage is like a three-speed gearbox: affection, friendship, love. It is not advisable to crash your gears and go right through to love straightaway. You need to ease your way through. The basis of love is respect, and that needs to be learned from affection and friendship.

—*Peter Ustinov*[2]

And the rib, which the LORD God had taken from man, made he a woman, and brought her unto the man.

And Adam said, This is now bone of my bones, and flesh of my flesh: she shall be called Woman, because she was taken out of Man.

Therefore shall a man leave his father and his mother, and shall cleave unto his wife: and they shall be one flesh.

And they were both naked, the man and his wife, and were not ashamed.

—*Genesis 2:15–25*

Two are better than one; because they have a good reward for their labour.

For if they fall, the one will lift up his fellow: but woe to him that is alone when he falleth; for he hath not another to help him up.

Again, if two lie together, then they have heat: but how can one be warm alone?

And if one prevail against him, two shall withstand him; and a threefold cord is not quickly broken.

—*Ecclesiastes 4:9–12*

Learn to Pray for One Another

I'd rather be able to pray than be a great preacher. Jesus Christ never taught his disciples how to preach, but only how to pray.

—*D. L. Moody*

And this I pray, that your love may abound yet more and more in knowledge and in all judgment.

—*Philippians 1:9*

For this cause we also, since the day we heard it, do not cease to pray for you, and to desire that ye might be filled with the knowledge of his will in all wisdom and spiritual understanding;

That ye might walk worthy of the Lord unto all pleasing, being fruitful in every good work, and increasing in the knowledge of God;

Strengthened with all might, according to his glorious power, unto all patience and longsuffering with joyfulness.

—Colossians 1:9–11

Reuben heard it, and he delivered [Joseph] out of their hands; and said, Let us not kill him.

And Reuben said unto them, Shed no blood, but cast him into this pit that is in the wilderness, and lay no hand upon him; that he might rid him out of their hands, to deliver him to his father again.

—Genesis 37:21–22

I beseech thee for my son Onesimus, whom I have begotten in my bonds:

Which in time past was to thee unprofitable, but now profitable to thee and to me:

—Philemon 10–11

Live by God's Spirit

O Holy Spirit, who in the hush of an upper room didst fall upon men and women like a rushing, mighty wind, purifying them as with flame, sending them out with a power beyond themselves, knit us in a close and loving fellowship that we too may receive thee.

—Leslie D. Weatherhead[3]

If ye then, being evil, know how to give good gifts unto your children: how much more shall your heavenly Father give the Holy Spirit to them that ask him?

—Luke 11:13

In the last day, that great day of the feast, Jesus stood and cried, saying, If any man thirst, let him come unto me, and drink.

He that believeth on me, as the scripture hath said, out of his belly shall flow rivers of living water.

(But this spake he of the Spirit, which they that believe on him should receive: for the Holy Ghost was not yet given; because that Jesus was not yet glorified.)

—John 7:37–39

37

And I will pray the Father, and he shall give you another Comforter, that he may abide with you for ever;

Even the Spirit of truth; whom the world cannot receive, because it seeth him not, neither knoweth him: but ye know him; for he dwelleth with you, and shall be in you.

—*John 14:16–17*

But the Comforter, which is the Holy Ghost, whom the Father will send in my name, he shall teach you all things, and bring all things to your remembrance, whatsoever I have said unto you.

Peace I leave with you, my peace I give unto you: not as the world giveth, give I unto you. Let not your heart be troubled, neither let it be afraid.

—*John 14:26–27*

But when the Comforter is come, whom I will send unto you from the Father, even the Spirit of truth, which proceedeth from the Father, he shall testify of me:

—*John 15:26*

Remind One Another of God's Blessings!

The more we understand that we are adopted as "special-needs children" by our Father in heaven, the more we will experience what Christian writer and speaker Brennan Manning refers to as a healing of our image of God. All of us need help with this healing; some, who have not had fathers growing up or who now have painful memories of their fathers, need more help in seeing God as "Abba, Father." As we understand and internalize our own adoption by God, as we realize that his choosing is based on his immense love for us, without regard for what we've done or accomplished, our image of God can begin to be healed.

—David V. Andersen[4]

Every good gift and every perfect gift is from above, and cometh down from the Father of lights, with whom is no variableness, neither shadow of turning.

Of his own will begat he us with the word of truth, that we should be a kind of firstfruits of his creatures.

—James 1:17–18

39

He turneth the wilderness into a standing water, and dry ground into watersprings.

And there he maketh the hungry to dwell, that they may prepare a city for habitation;

And sow the fields, and plant vineyards, which may yield fruits of increase.

He blesseth them also, so that they are multiplied greatly; and suffereth not their cattle to decrease.

—*Psalm 107:35–38*

The righteous shall flourish like the palm tree: he shall grow like a cedar in Lebanon.

Those that be planted in the house of the LORD shall flourish in the courts of our God.

They shall still bring forth fruit in old age; they shall be fat and flourishing.

—*Psalm 92:12–14*

Blessed be the God and Father of our Lord Jesus Christ, who hath blessed us with all spiritual blessings in heavenly places in Christ:

According as he hath chosen us in him before the foundation of the world, that we should be holy and without blame before him in love:

Having predestinated us unto the adoption of children by Jesus Christ to himself, according to the good pleasure of his will,

To the praise of the glory of his grace, wherein he hath made us accepted in the beloved.

In whom we have redemption through his blood, the forgiveness of sins, according to the riches of his grace;

Wherein he hath abounded toward us in all wisdom and prudence;

Having made known unto us the mystery of his will, according to his good pleasure which he hath purposed in himself:

That in the dispensation of the fulness of times he might gather together in one all things in Christ, both which are in heaven, and which are on earth; even in him:

In whom also we have obtained an inheritance, being predestinated according to the purpose of him who worketh all things after the counsel of his own will:

That we should be to the praise of his glory, who first trusted in Christ.

In whom ye also trusted, after that ye heard the word of truth, the gospel of your salvation:

in whom also after that ye believed, ye were sealed with that holy Spirit of promise,

Which is the earnest of our inheritance until the redemption of the purchased possession, unto the praise of his glory.

—*Ephesians 1:3–14*

Strengthened with all might, according to his glorious power, unto all patience and longsuffering with joyfulness;

Giving thanks unto the Father, which hath made us meet to be partakers of the inheritance of the saints in light.

—*Colossians 1:11–12*

— Three —

Enjoying Family Life

Yes, family life is supposed to be enjoyable! How has it been lately?
When the pressures of our hectic schedules push our enjoyment of one another to the periphery, it's time to slow down and let the promises of God speak anew. After all, He is right in the midst of our families, too—waiting to be noticed, extending His peace and comfort.

When You're Tense and Stressed-Out at Home

As sure as ever God puts his children in the furnace, he will be in the furnace with them.

—*Charles Spurgeon*

All things are for your sakes, that the abundant grace might through the thanksgiving of many redound to the glory of God.

For which cause we faint not; but though our outward man perish, yet the inward man is renewed day by day.

For our light affliction, which is but for a moment, worketh for us a far more exceeding and eternal weight of glory;

While we look not at the things which are seen, but at the things which are not seen: for the things which are seen are temporal; but the things which are not seen are eternal.

—*2 Corinthians 4:15–18*

I waited patiently for the LORD; and he inclined unto me, and heard my cry.

He brought me up also out of an horrible pit, out of the miry clay, and set my feet upon a rock, and established my goings.

And he hath put a new song in my mouth, even praise unto our God: many shall see it, and fear, and shall trust in the LORD.

—Psalm 40:1–3

Truly my soul waiteth upon God: from him cometh my salvation.

He only is my rock and my salvation; he is my defence; I shall not be greatly moved.

—Psalm 62:1–2

In the day of my trouble I sought the Lord: my sore ran in the night, and ceased not: my soul refused to be comforted.

I remembered God, and was troubled: I complained, and my spirit was overwhelmed. Selah.

Thou holdest mine eyes waking: I am so troubled that I cannot speak.

I have considered the days of old, the years of ancient times.

I call to remembrance my song in the night: I commune with mine own heart: and my spirit made diligent search.

—*Psalm 77:2–6*

O LORD, thou knowest: remember me, and visit me, and revenge me of my persecutors; take me not away in thy longsuffering: know that for thy sake I have suffered rebuke.

Thy words were found, and I did eat them; and thy word was unto me the joy and rejoicing of mine heart: for I am called by thy name, O LORD God of hosts.

—*Jeremiah 15:15–16*

Who shall also confirm you unto the end, that ye may be blameless in the day of our Lord Jesus Christ.

God is faithful, by whom ye were called unto the fellowship of his Son Jesus Christ our Lord.

—*1 Corinthians 1:8–9*

Rejoice evermore.

Pray without ceasing.

In every thing give thanks: for this is the will of God in Christ Jesus concerning you.

—1 Thessalonians 5:16–18

Show Hospitality toward Others

You cannot do a kindness too soon, because you never know how soon it will be too late.

—Source Unknown

He that receiveth a prophet in the name of a prophet shall receive a prophet's reward; and he that receiveth a righteous man in the name of a righteous man shall receive a righteous man's reward.

And whosoever shall give to drink unto one of these little ones a cup of cold water only in the name of a disciple, verily I say unto you, he shall in no wise lose his reward.

—Matthew 10:41–42

Then said he also to him that bade him, When thou makest a dinner or a supper, call not thy friends, nor thy brethren, neither thy kinsmen, nor thy rich neighbours; lest they also bid thee again, and a recompence be made thee.

But when thou makest a feast, call the poor, the maimed, the lame, the blind:

And thou shalt be blessed; for they cannot recompense thee: for thou shalt be recompensed at the resurrection of the just.

—Luke 14:12–14

Then Peter went down to the men which were sent unto him from Cornelius; and said, Behold, I am he whom ye seek: what is the cause wherefore ye are come?

And they said, Cornelius the centurion, a just man, and one that feareth God, and of good report among all the nation of the Jews, was warned from God by an holy angel to send for thee into his house, and to hear words of thee.

Then called he them in, and lodged them. And on the morrow Peter went away with them, and certain brethren from Joppa accompanied him.

—Acts 10:21–23

And when they were escaped, then they knew that the island was called Melita.

And the barbarous people shewed us no little kindness: for they kindled a fire, and received us every one, because of the present rain, and because of the cold.

—*Acts 28:1–2*

Beloved, thou doest faithfully whatsoever thou doest to the brethren, and to strangers;

Which have borne witness of thy charity before the church: whom if thou bring forward on their journey after a godly sort, thou shalt do well:

Because that for his name's sake they went forth, taking nothing of the Gentiles.

We therefore ought to receive such, that we might be fellowhelpers to the truth.

—*3 John 5–8*

Lead Your Children in God's Ways

An important thing for parents to teach their children is how to get along without them.
—*Frances Clark*

Bring them up in the nurture and admonition of the Lord.
—*Ephesians 6:4b*

Train up a child in the way he should go: and when he is old, he will not depart from it.
—*Proverbs 22:6*

Only take heed to thyself, and keep thy soul diligently, lest thou forget the things which thine eyes have seen, and lest they depart from thy heart all the days of thy life: but teach them thy sons, and thy sons' sons;

Specially the day that thou stoodest before the LORD thy God in Horeb, when the LORD said unto me, Gather me the people together, and I will make them hear my words, that they may learn to fear me all the days that they shall live upon the earth, and that they may teach their children.
—*Deuteronomy 4:9–10*

And these words, which I command thee this day, shall be in thine heart:

And thou shalt teach them diligently unto thy children, and shalt talk of them when thou sittest in thine house, and when thou walkest by the way, and when thou liest down, and when thou risest up.

And thou shalt bind them for a sign upon thine hand, and they shall be as frontlets between thine eyes.

And thou shalt write them upon the posts of thy house, and on thy gates.

—*Deuteronomy 6:6–9*

And ye shall teach them your children, speaking of them when thou sittest in thine house, and when thou walkest by the way, when thou liest down, and when thou risest up.

—*Deuteronomy 11:19*

Correct thy son, and he shall give thee rest; yea, he shall give delight unto thy soul.

—*Proverbs 29:17*

♥ *Guide Them with God's Wisdom*

Children, obey your parents in all things: for this is well pleasing unto the Lord.

—*Colossians 3:20*

Ye shall fear every man his mother, and his father, and keep my sabbaths: I am the LORD your God.

—*Leviticus 19:3*

My son, if thou wilt receive my words, and hide my commandments with thee;

So that thou incline thine ear unto wisdom, and apply thine heart to understanding;

Yea, if thou criest after knowledge, and liftest up thy voice for understanding;

If thou seekest her as silver, and searchest for her as for hid treasures;

Then shalt thou understand the fear of the LORD, and find the knowledge of God.

—*Proverbs 2:1–5*

He is in the way of life that keepeth instruction: but he that refuseth reproof erreth.

—Proverbs 10:17

Whoso despiseth the word shall be destroyed: but he that feareth the commandment shall be rewarded.

—Proverbs 13:13

Honour thy father and thy mother, as the LORD thy God hath commanded thee; that thy days may be prolonged, and that it may go well with thee, in the land which the LORD thy God giveth thee.

—Deuteronomy 5:16

My son, if thine heart be wise, my heart shall rejoice, even mine.

Yea, my reins shall rejoice, when thy lips speak right things.

Let not thine heart envy sinners: but be thou in the fear of the LORD all the day long.

For surely there is an end; and thine expectation shall not be cut off.

Hear thou, my son, and be wise, and guide thine heart in the way.

Be not among winebibbers; among riotous eaters of flesh:

For the drunkard and the glutton shall come to poverty: and drowsiness shall clothe a man with rags.

Hearken unto thy father that begat thee, and despise not thy mother when she is old.

Buy the truth, and sell it not; also wisdom, and instruction, and understanding.

The father of the righteous shall greatly rejoice: and he that begetteth a wise child shall have joy of him.

Thy father and thy mother shall be glad, and she that bare thee shall rejoice.

My son, give me thine heart, and let thine eyes observe my ways.

—*Proverbs 23:15–26*

❤ *Provide Loving Discipline*

Withhold not correction from the child: for if thou beatest him with the rod, he shall not die.

—*Proverbs 23:13*

Now the sons of Eli were sons of Belial; they knew not the LORD.

And the priest's custom with the people was, that, when any man offered sacrifice, the priest's servant came, while the flesh was in seething, with a fleshhook of three teeth in his hand;

And he struck it into the pan, or kettle, or caldron, or pot; all that the fleshhook brought up the priest took for himself. So they did in Shiloh unto all the Israelites that came thither.

Also before they burnt the fat, the priest's servant came, and said to the man that sacrificed, Give flesh to roast for the priest; for he will not have sodden flesh of thee, but raw.

And if any man said unto him, Let them not fail to burn the fat presently, and then take as much as thy soul desireth; then he would answer him, Nay; but thou shalt give it me now: and if not, I will take it by force.

Wherefore the sin of the young men was very great before the LORD: for men abhorred the offering of the LORD.

But Samuel ministered before the LORD, being a child, girded with a linen ephod.

Moreover his mother made him a little coat, and brought it to him from year to year, when she came up with her husband to offer the yearly sacrifice.

And Eli blessed Elkanah and his wife, and said, The LORD give thee seed of this woman for the loan which is lent to the LORD. And they went unto their own home.

And the LORD visited Hannah, so that she conceived, and bare three sons and two daughters. And the child Samuel grew before the LORD.

Now Eli was very old, and heard all that his sons did unto all Israel; and how they lay with the women that assembled at the door of the tabernacle of the congregation.

And he said unto them, Why do ye such things? for I hear of your evil dealings by all this people.

Nay, my sons; for it is no good report that I hear: ye make the LORD's people to transgress.

If one man sin against another, the judge shall judge him: but if a man sin against the LORD, who shall intreat for him? Notwithstanding they hearkened not unto the voice of their father, because the LORD would slay them.

—1 Samuel 2:12–25

56

Correct thy son, and he shall give thee rest; yea, he shall give delight unto thy soul.

—*Proverbs 29:17*

Ye have forgotten the exhortation which speaketh unto you as unto children, My son, despise not thou the chastening of the Lord, nor faint when thou art rebuked of him:

For whom the Lord loveth he chasteneth, and scourgeth every son whom he receiveth.

If ye endure chastening, God dealeth with you as with sons; for what son is he whom the father chasteneth not?

But if ye be without chastisement, whereof all are partakers, then are ye bastards, and not sons.

Furthermore we have had fathers of our flesh which corrected us, and we gave them reverence: shall we not much rather be in subjection unto the Father of spirits, and live?

For they verily for a few days chastened us after their own pleasure; but he for our profit, that we might be partakers of his holiness.

Now no chastening for the present seemeth to be joyous, but grievous: nevertheless afterward it yieldeth the peaceable fruit of righteousness unto them which are exercised thereby.

—*Hebrews 12:5–11*

He that spareth his rod hateth his son: but he that loveth him chasteneth him betimes.

—*Proverbs 13:24*

Respect Your In-Laws!

The awe and dread with which the untutored savage contemplates his mother-in-law are amongst the most familiar facts of anthropology.

—*Sir James George Frazer* [1]

It came to pass on the morrow, that Moses sat to judge the people: and the people stood by Moses from the morning unto the evening.

And when Moses' father in law saw all that he did to the people, he said, What is this thing that thou doest to the people? why sittest thou thyself alone, and all the people stand by thee from morning unto even?

And Moses said unto his father in law, Because the people come unto me to enquire of God:

When they have a matter, they come unto me; and I judge between one and another,

58

and I do make them know the statutes of God, and his laws.

And Moses' father in law said unto him, The thing that thou doest is not good.

Thou wilt surely wear away, both thou, and this people that is with thee: for this thing is too heavy for thee; thou art not able to perform it thyself alone.

Hearken now unto my voice, I will give thee counsel, and God shall be with thee: Be thou for the people to God-ward, that thou mayest bring the causes unto God:

And thou shalt teach them ordinances and laws, and shalt shew them the way wherein they must walk, and the work that they must do.

Moreover thou shalt provide out of all the people able men, such as fear God, men of truth, hating covetousness; and place such over them, to be rulers of thousands, and rulers of hundreds, rulers of fifties, and rulers of tens.

And let them judge the people at all seasons: and it shall be, that every great matter they shall bring unto thee, but every small matter they shall judge: so shall it be easier for thyself, and they shall bear the burden with thee.

If thou shalt do this thing, and God command thee so, then thou shalt be able to endure, and all this people shall also go to their place in peace.

So Moses hearkened to the voice of his father in law, and did all that he had said.

—*Exodus 18:13–24*

Then she arose with her daughters in law, that she might return from the country of Moab: for she had heard in the country of Moab how that the LORD had visited his people in giving them bread.

Wherefore she went forth out of the place where she was, and her two daughters in law with her; and they went on the way to return unto the land of Judah.

And Naomi said unto her two daughters in law, Go, return each to her mother's house: the LORD deal kindly with you, as ye have dealt with the dead, and with me.

The LORD grant you that ye may find rest, each of you in the house of her husband. Then she kissed them; and they lifted up their voice, and wept.

And they said unto her, Surely we will return with thee unto thy people.

And Naomi said, Turn again, my daughters: why will ye go with me? are there yet any more sons in my womb, that they may be your husbands?

Turn again, my daughters, go your way; for I am too old to have an husband. If I should say, I have hope, if I should have an husband also to night, and should also bear sons;

Would ye tarry for them till they were grown? would ye stay for them from having husbands? nay, my daughters; for it grieveth me much for your sakes that the hand of the LORD is gone out against me.

And they lifted up their voice, and wept again: and Orpah kissed her mother in law; but Ruth clave unto her.

And she said, Behold, thy sister in law is gone back unto her people, and unto her gods: return thou after thy sister in law.

And Ruth said, Intreat me not to leave thee, or to return from following after thee: for whither thou goest, I will go; and where thou lodgest, I will lodge: thy people shall be my people, and thy God my God:

Where thou diest, will I die, and there will I be buried: the LORD do so to me, and more also, if ought but death part thee and me.

When she saw that she was stedfastly minded to go with her, then she left speaking unto her.

—*Ruth 1:6–18*

Four

Seeking Fellowship in the Church

It's not enough just to have one another. We were made for a broader and fuller life of fellowship with all of God's children. For we shall dwell in eternity with all who know and love Him. Let's prepare now by learning to know and love our brothers and sisters in the church. The first step is a commitment to being there, regularly, for worship and prayer together.

Enjoy Fellowship in the Church

If absence makes the heart grow fonder, some people ought to love their church greatly.
—*Anonymous*

By the rivers of Babylon, there we sat down, yea, we wept, when we remembered Zion.

We hanged our harps upon the willows in the midst thereof.

For there they that carried us away captive required of us a song; and they that wasted us required of us mirth, saying, Sing us one of the songs of Zion.

How shall we sing the LORD's song in a strange land?

If I forget thee, O Jerusalem, let my right hand forget her cunning.

If I do not remember thee, let my tongue cleave to the roof of my mouth; if I prefer not Jerusalem above my chief joy.

—*Psalm 137:1–6*

And let us consider one another to provoke unto love and to good works:

Not forsaking the assembling of ourselves together, as the manner of some is; but exhorting one another: and so much the more, as ye see the day approaching.

—*Hebrews 10:24–25*

I am the vine, ye are the branches: He that abideth in me, and I in him, the same bringeth forth much fruit: for without me ye can do nothing.

If a man abide not in me, he is cast forth as a branch, and is withered; and men gather them, and cast them into the fire, and they are burned.

—*John 15:5–6*

Two are better than one; because they have a good reward for their labour.

For if they fall, the one will lift up his fellow: but woe to him that is alone when he falleth; for he hath not another to help him up.

Again, if two lie together, then they have heat: but how can one be warm alone?

And if one prevail against him, two shall withstand him; and a threefold cord is not quickly broken.

—Ecclesiastes 4:9–12

Behold, two of them went that same day to a village called Emmaus, which was from Jerusalem about threescore furlongs.

And they talked together of all these things which had happened.

And it came to pass, that, while they communed together and reasoned, Jesus himself drew near, and went with them.

—Luke 24:13–15

And they continued stedfastly in the apostles' doctrine and fellowship, and in breaking of bread, and in prayers.

And fear came upon every soul: and many wonders and signs were done by the apostles.

And all that believed were together, and had all things common;

And sold their possessions and goods, and parted them to all men, as every man had need.

And they, continuing daily with one accord in the temple, and breaking bread from house to house, did eat their meat with gladness and singleness of heart,

Praising God, and having favour with all the people. And the Lord added to the church daily such as should be saved.

—Acts 2:42–47

We then that are strong ought to bear the infirmities of the weak, and not to please ourselves.

Let every one of us please his neighbour for his good to edification.

For even Christ pleased not himself; but, as it is written, The reproaches of them that reproached thee fell on me.

For whatsoever things were written aforetime were written for our learning, that we through patience and comfort of the scriptures might have hope.

Now the God of patience and consolation grant you to be likeminded one toward another according to Christ Jesus:

That ye may with one mind and one mouth glorify God, even the Father of our Lord Jesus Christ.

Wherefore receive ye one another, as Christ also received us to the glory of God.

—*Romans 15:1–7*

For ye are all the children of God by faith in Christ Jesus.

For as many of you as have been baptized into Christ have put on Christ.

There is neither Jew nor Greek, there is neither bond nor free, there is neither male nor female: for ye are all one in Christ Jesus.

—*Galatians 3:26–28*

Experience Brotherly Love

The disciples call upon the heavenly Father as a corporate body. They call upon a Father who already knows his children's needs. The call of Jesus binds them into a brotherhood. In Jesus they have apprehended the lovingkindness of the Father. In the name of the Son of God they are privileged to call God Father. They are on earth, and their Father is in heaven. He looks down on them from above, and they lift up their eyes to him.

— *Dietrich Bonhoeffer[1]*

But as touching brotherly love ye need not that I write unto you: for ye yourselves are taught of God to love one another.

And indeed ye do it toward all the brethren which are in all Macedonia: but we beseech you, brethren, that ye increase more and more;

And that ye study to be quiet, and to do your own business, and to work with your own hands, as we commanded you;

That ye may walk honestly toward them that are without, and that ye may have lack of nothing.

—1 Thessalonians 4:9–12

And beside this, giving all diligence, add to your faith virtue; and to virtue knowledge;

And to knowledge temperance; and to temperance patience; and to patience godliness;

And to godliness brotherly kindness; and to brotherly kindness charity.

For if these things be in you, and abound, they make you that ye shall neither be barren nor unfruitful in the knowledge of our Lord Jesus Christ.

But he that lacketh these things is blind, and cannot see afar off, and hath forgotten that he was purged from his old sins.

—2 Peter 1:5–9

Respect Your Pastors and Church Leaders . . .

The pastor today is the man on the hot seat. He is supposed to be the man who can do everything. He is supposed to be the visionary for the church. He has to be a strong leader with good business and administrative skills. He has to be entertaining and produce a very thought-provoking sermon every week. He's often in charge of the financial aspects of the church. He's usually responsible for counseling church members with complex personal problems that he may not be equipped to handle. He has to visit the sick and families in which someone has died. He has to preach the funerals and perform the weddings. It's an impossible assignment! It's built for burnout, it's built for exhaustion, and it's built for trouble.

—James Dobson[2]

We beseech you, brethren, to know them which labour among you, and are over you in the Lord, and admonish you;

And to esteem them very highly in love for their work's sake. And be at peace among yourselves.

—1 Thessalonians 5:12–13

Remember them which have the rule over you, who have spoken unto you the word of God: whose faith follow, considering the end of their conversation. . . .

Obey them that have the rule over you, and submit yourselves: for they watch for your souls, as they that must give account, that they may do it with joy, and not with grief: for that is unprofitable for you.

—Hebrews 13:7, 17

Put them in mind to be subject to principalities and powers, to obey magistrates, to be ready to every good work,

To speak evil of no man, to be no brawlers, but gentle, shewing all meekness unto all men.

—Titus 3:1–2

Be ye followers of me, even as I also am of Christ.

Now I praise you, brethren, that ye remember me in all things, and keep the ordinances, as I delivered them to you.

—*1 Corinthians 11:1–2*

I beseech you, brethren, (ye know the house of Stephanas, that it is the firstfruits of Achaia, and that they have addicted themselves to the ministry of the saints,)

That ye submit yourselves unto such, and to every one that helpeth with us, and laboureth.

—*1 Corinthians 16:15–16*

❤ *Remember: They Are Called by God*

And no man taketh this honour unto himself, but he that is called of God, as was Aaron.

—*Hebrews 5:4*

He saith to him again the second time, Simon, son of Jonas, lovest thou me? He saith unto him, Yea, Lord; thou knowest that I love thee. He saith unto him, Feed my sheep.

He saith unto him the third time, Simon, son of Jonas, lovest thou me? Peter was grieved because he said unto him the third time, Lovest thou me? And he said unto him, Lord, thou knowest all things; thou knowest that I love thee. Jesus saith unto him, Feed my sheep.

Verily, verily, I say unto thee, When thou wast young, thou girdedst thyself, and walkedst whither thou wouldest: but when thou shalt be old, thou shalt stretch forth thy hands, and another shall gird thee, and carry thee whither thou wouldest not.

—*John 21:16–18*

For the which cause I also suffer these things: nevertheless I am not ashamed: for I know whom I have believed, and am persuaded that he is able to keep that which I have committed unto him against that day.

Hold fast the form of sound words, which thou hast heard of me, in faith and love which is in Christ Jesus.

That good thing which was committed unto thee keep by the Holy Ghost which dwelleth in us.

—*2 Timothy 1:12–14*

But hath in due times manifested his word through preaching, which is committed unto me according to the commandment of God our Saviour.

—*Titus 1:3*

❤ *Accept Them as Your Examples*

Though the Lord give you the bread of adversity, and the water of affliction, yet shall not thy teachers be removed into a corner any more, but thine eyes shall see thy teachers.

—*Isaiah 30:20*

Brethren, be followers together of me, and mark them which walk so as ye have us for an ensample.

—*Philippians 3:17*

Not because we have not power, but to make ourselves an ensample unto you to follow us.

—*2 Thessalonians 3:9*

Neither as being lords over God's heritage, but being ensamples to the flock.

—*1 Peter 5:3*

❤ *Show Hospitality to Your Pastor*

The next day we that were of Paul's company departed, and came unto Caesarea: and we entered into the house of Philip the evangelist, which was one of the seven; and abode with him.

And the same man had four daughters, virgins, which did prophesy.

And as we tarried there many days, there came down from Judaea a certain prophet, named Agabus.

—*Acts 21:8–10*

75

❤ *Pray for Your Pastor!*

Brethren, pray for us.

—1 Thessalonians 5:25

Then saith he unto his disciples, The harvest truly is plenteous, but the labourers are few;

Pray ye therefore the Lord of the harvest, that he will send forth labourers into his harvest.

—Matthew 9:37–38

Whom they set before the apostles: and when they had prayed, they laid their hands on them.

—Acts 6:6

Now I beseech you, brethren, for the Lord Jesus Christ's sake, and for the love of the Spirit, that ye strive together with me in your prayers to God for me;

That I may be delivered from them that do not believe in Judaea; and that my service which I have for Jerusalem may be accepted of the saints;

That I may come unto you with joy by the will of God, and may with you be refreshed.

—Romans 15:30–32

Praying always with all prayer and supplication in the Spirit, and watching thereunto with all perseverance and supplication for all saints;

And for me, that utterance may be given unto me, that I may open my mouth boldly, to make known the mystery of the gospel,

For which I am an ambassador in bonds: that therein I may speak boldly, as I ought to speak.

—Ephesians 6:18–20

Continue in prayer, and watch in the same with thanksgiving;

Withal praying also for us, that God would open unto us a door of utterance, to speak the mystery of Christ, for which I am also in bonds:

That I may make it manifest, as I ought to speak.

—Colossians 4:2–4

Finally, brethren, pray for us, that the word of the Lord may have free course, and be glorified, even as it is with you:

And that we may be delivered from unreasonable and wicked men: for all men have not faith.

—2 Thessalonians 3:1–2

Pray for us: for we trust we have a good conscience, in all things willing to live honestly.

But I beseech you the rather to do this, that I may be restored to you the sooner.

—Hebrews 13:18–19

❤ Beware of False and Corrupt Ministers

Beloved, believe not every spirit, but try the spirits whether they are of God: because many false prophets are gone out into the world.

Hereby know ye the Spirit of God: Every spirit that confesseth that Jesus Christ is come in the flesh is of God:

And every spirit that confesseth not that Jesus Christ is come in the flesh is not of God: and this is that spirit of antichrist, whereof ye have heard that it should come; and even now already is it in the world.

Ye are of God, little children, and have overcome them: because greater is he that is in you, than he that is in the world.

They are of the world: therefore speak they of the world, and the world heareth them.

—*1 John 4:1–5*

For many deceivers are entered into the world, who confess not that Jesus Christ is come in the flesh. This is a deceiver and an antichrist.

Look to yourselves, that we lose not those things which we have wrought, but that we receive a full reward.

Whosoever transgresseth, and abideth not in the doctrine of Christ, hath not God. He that abideth in the doctrine of Christ, he hath both the Father and the Son.

If there come any unto you, and bring not this doctrine, receive him not into your house, neither bid him God speed:

—*2 John 7–10*

Discover and Exercise Your Spiritual Gifts

For the real good of every gift it is essential, first, that the giver be in the gift—as God always is, for He is love—and next, that the receiver know and receive the giver in the gift. Every gift of God is but a harbinger of His greatest and only sufficing gift—that of Himself.

—George MacDonald

For the body is not one member but many.

If the foot shall say, Because I am not the hand, I am not of the body; is it therefore not of the body?

And if the ear shall say, Because I am not the eye, I am not of the body; is it therefore not of the body?

If the whole body were an eye, where were the hearing? If the whole were hearing, where were the smelling?

But now hath God set the members every one of them in the body, as it hath pleased him.

And if they were all one member, where were the body?

But now are they many members, yet but one body.

And the eye cannot say unto the hand, I have no need of thee: nor again the head to the feet, I have no need of you.

Nay, much more those members of the body, which seem to be more feeble, are necessary:

And those members of the body, which we think to be less honourable, upon these we bestow more abundant honour; and our uncomely parts have more abundant comeliness.

For our comely parts have no need: but God hath tempered the body together, having given more abundant honour to that part which lacked:

That there should be no schism in the body; but that the members should have the same care one for another.

And whether one member suffer, all the members suffer with it; or one member be honoured, all the members rejoice with it.

—1 Corinthians 12:14–26

Now ye are the body of Christ, and members in particular.

And God hath set some in the church, first apostles, secondarily prophets, thirdly teachers, after that miracles, then gifts of healings, helps, governments, diversities of tongues.

Are all apostles? are all prophets? are all teachers? are all workers of miracles?

Have all the gifts of healing? do all speak with tongues? do all interpret?

But covet earnestly the best gifts: and yet shew I unto you a more excellent way.

—*1 Corinthians 12:27–31*

And he gave some, apostles; and some, prophets; and some, evangelists; and some, pastors and teachers;

For the perfecting of the saints, for the work of the ministry, for the edifying of the body of Christ.

—*Ephesians 4:11–12*

As every man hath received the gift, even so minister the same one to another, as good stewards of the manifold grace of God.

If any man speak, let him speak as the oracles of God; if any man minister, let him do it as of the ability which God giveth: that God in all things may be glorified through Jesus Christ, to whom be praise and dominion for ever and ever. Amen.

—*1 Peter 4:10–11*

— F i v e —

Seeking God's Guidance for Your Family

It's a responsibility of everyone, but especially of parents, to know God and seek His best for the family. But it's also a relief to know that the burden is not entirely upon us. For God already wants the very best for our family. If we will simply let Him guide, we'll enjoy the richest of His blessings.

Commit to Doing God's Will

There was a pious old gentleman of an earlier generation who used to get up regularly at prayer meeting in his church to pray: "Use me, O Lord, use me—in some advisory capacity!"

—James Hewett[1]

Thus saith the LORD the King of Israel, and his redeemer the LORD of hosts; I am the first, and I am the last; and beside me there is no God.

—Isaiah 44:6

I beseech you therefore, brethren, by the mercies of God, that ye present your bodies a living sacrifice, holy, acceptable unto God, which is your reasonable service.

—Romans 12:1

And Abel, he also brought of the firstlings of his flock and of the fat thereof. And the LORD had respect unto Abel and to his offering:

But unto Cain and to his offering he had not respect. And Cain was very wroth, and his countenance fell.

And the LORD said unto Cain, Why art thou wroth? and why is thy countenance fallen?

If thou doest well, shalt thou not be accepted? and if thou doest not well, sin lieth at the door.

—Genesis 4:4–7a

Again, the kingdom of heaven is like unto treasure hid in a field; the which when a man hath found, he hideth, and for joy thereof goeth and selleth all that he hath, and buyeth that field.

Again, the kingdom of heaven is like unto a merchant man, seeking goodly pearls:

Who, when he had found one pearl of great price, went and sold all that he had, and bought it.

—Matthew 13:44–46

And this they did, not as we hoped, but first gave their own selves to the Lord, and unto us by the will of God.

—2 Corinthians 8:5

♥ *Pursue God's Wisdom*

I am thy servant; give me understanding, that I may know thy testimonies.

—Psalm 119:125

The fear of the LORD is the beginning of wisdom: a good understanding have all they that do his commandments: his praise endureth for ever.

—Psalm 111:10

If any of you lack wisdom, let him ask of God, that giveth to all men liberally, and upbraideth not; and it shall be given him.

But let him ask in faith, nothing wavering. For he that wavereth is like a wave of the sea driven with the wind and tossed.

For let not that man think that he shall receive any thing of the Lord.

A double minded man is unstable in all his ways.

—James 1:5–8

When they bring you unto the synagogues, and unto magistrates, and powers, take ye no thought how or what thing ye shall answer, or what ye shall say:

For the Holy Ghost shall teach you in the same hour what ye ought to say.

—Luke 12:11–12

For I will give you a mouth and wisdom, which all your adversaries shall not be able to gainsay nor resist.

—Luke 21:15

Consider what I say; and the Lord give thee understanding in all things.

—2 Timothy 2:7

We know that the Son of God is come, and hath given us an understanding, that we may know him that is true, and we are in him that is true, even in his Son Jesus Christ. This is the true God, and eternal life.

—1 John 5:20

❤ *Pray Daily for Guidance*

Thy word is a lamp unto my feet, and a light unto my path. . . .

I am thy servant; give me understanding, that I may know thy testimonies.

—*Psalm 119:105, 125*

Man's goings are of the LORD; how can a man then understand his own way?

—*Proverbs 20:24*

Thus saith the LORD, thy Redeemer, the Holy One of Israel; I am the LORD thy God which teacheth thee to profit, which leadeth thee by the way that thou shouldest go.

O that thou hadst hearkened to my commandments! then had thy peace been as a river, and thy righteousness as the waves of the sea.

—*Isaiah 49:10–11*

They shall not hunger nor thirst; neither shall the heat nor sun smite them: for he that hath mercy on them shall lead them, even by the springs of water shall he guide them.

And I will make all my mountains a way, and my highways shall be exalted.

—*Isaiah 49:11–12*

A new heart also will I give you, and a new spirit will I put within you: and I will take away the stony heart out of your flesh, and I will give you an heart of flesh.

And I will put my spirit within you, and cause you to walk in my statutes, and ye shall keep my judgments, and do them.

—*Ezekiel 36:26–27*

Behold, the days come, saith the Lord GOD, that I will send a famine in the land, not a famine of bread, nor a thirst for water, but of hearing the words of the LORD:

And they shall wander from sea to sea, and from the north even to the east, they shall run to and fro to seek the word of the LORD, and shall not find it.

—*Amos 8:11–12*

And Israel took his journey with all that he had, and came to Beer-sheba, and offered sacrifices unto the God of his father Isaac.

And God spake unto Israel in the visions of the night, and said, Jacob, Jacob. And he said, Here am I.

And he said, I am God, the God of thy father: fear not to go down into Egypt; for I will there make of thee a great nation:

I will go down with thee into Egypt; and I will also surely bring thee up again: and Joseph shall put his hand upon thine eyes.

—*Genesis 46:1–4*

It came to pass after this, that David enquired of the LORD, saying, Shall I go up into any of the cities of Judah? And the LORD said unto him, Go up. And David said, Whither shall I go up? And he said, Unto Hebron.

So David went up thither, and his two wives also, Ahinoam the Jezreelitess, and Abigail Nabal's wife the Carmelite.

And his men that were with him did David bring up, every man with his household: and they dwelt in the cities of Hebron.

91

And the men of Judah came, and there they anointed David king over the house of Judah. And they told David, saying, That the men of Jabesh-gilead were they that buried Saul.

—*2 Samuel 2:1–4*

Now there were in the church that was at Antioch certain prophets and teachers; as Barnabas, and Simeon that was called Niger, and Lucius of Cyrene, and Manaen, which had been brought up with Herod the tetrarch, and Saul.

As they ministered to the Lord, and fasted, the Holy Ghost said, Separate me Barnabas and Saul for the work whereunto I have called them.

And when they had fasted and prayed, and laid their hands on them, they sent them away.

—*Acts 13:1–3*

Then spake the Lord to Paul in the night by a vision, Be not afraid, but speak, and hold not thy peace:

For I am with thee, and no man shall set on thee to hurt thee: for I have much people in this city.

And he continued there a year and six months, teaching the word of God among them.

—*Acts 18:9–11*

Build Your Home on the Firmest Foundation

Most gracious Father,
this is our home;
Let your peace rest upon it.
let love abide here
love of one another,
love of mankind,
love of life itself,
and love of God.
Let us remember that
as many hands build a house,
so many hearts make a home.

—*Hugh Blackburne[2]*

Through wisdom is an house builded; and by understanding it is established.

—*Proverbs 24:3*

And wisdom and knowledge shall be the stability of thy times, and strength of salvation: the fear of the LORD is his treasure.

—*Isaiah 33:6*

Therefore whosoever heareth these sayings of mine, and doeth them, I will liken him unto a wise man, which built his house upon a rock:

And the rain descended, and the floods came, and the winds blew, and beat upon that house; and it fell not: for it was founded upon a rock.

And every one that heareth these sayings of mine, and doeth them not, shall be likened unto a foolish man, which built his house upon the sand:

And the rain descended, and the floods came, and the winds blew, and beat upon that house; and it fell: and great was the fall of it.

And it came to pass, when Jesus had ended these sayings, the people were astonished at his doctrine.

—*Matthew 7:24–28*

Yea, so have I strived to preach the gospel, not where Christ was named, lest I should build upon another man's foundation.

—*Romans 15:20*

For other foundation can no man lay than that is laid, which is Jesus Christ.

Now if any man build upon this foundation gold, silver, precious stones, wood, hay, stubble;

Every man's work shall be made manifest: for the day shall declare it, because it shall be revealed by fire; and the fire shall try every man's work of what sort it is.

If any man's work abide which he hath built thereupon, he shall receive a reward.

—*1 Corinthians 3:11–14*

Be not thou therefore ashamed of the testimony of our Lord, nor of me his prisoner: but be thou partaker of the afflictions of the gospel according to the power of God;

Who hath saved us, and called us with an holy calling, not according to our works, but according to his own purpose and grace, which was given us in Christ Jesus before the world began,

But is now made manifest by the appearing of our Saviour Jesus Christ, who hath abolished death, and hath brought life and immortality to light through the gospel.

—*2 Timothy 1:8–10*

Paul, a servant of God, and an apostle of Jesus Christ, according to the faith of God's elect, and the acknowledging of the truth which is after godliness;

In hope of eternal life, which God, that cannot lie, promised before the world began;

But hath in due times manifested his word through preaching, which is committed unto me according to the commandment of God our Saviour.

—*Titus 1:1–3*

I am Alpha and Omega, the beginning and the ending, saith the Lord, which is, and which was, and which is to come, the Almighty. . . . I am he that liveth, and was dead; and, behold, I am alive for evermore, Amen; and have the keys of hell and of death.

—*Revelation 1:8, 18*

❤ *Put God First in Your Family*

Honour the LORD with thy substance, and with the firstfruits of all thine increase:

So shall thy barns be filled with plenty, and thy presses shall burst out with new wine.

—Proverbs 3:9–10

The LORD maketh poor, and maketh rich: he bringeth low, and lifteth up.

He raiseth up the poor out of the dust, and lifteth up the beggar from the dunghill, to set them among princes, and to make them inherit the throne of glory: for the pillars of the earth are the LORD's, and he hath set the world upon them.

He will keep the feet of his saints, and the wicked shall be silent in darkness; for by strength shall no man prevail.

—1 Samuel 2:7–9

Lay not up for yourselves treasures upon earth, where moth and rust doth corrupt, and where thieves break through and steal:

But lay up for yourselves treasures in heaven, where neither moth nor rust doth corrupt, and where thieves do not break through nor steal:

For where your treasure is, there will your heart be also.

—Matthew 6:19–21

But godliness with contentment is great gain.

For we brought nothing into this world, and it is certain we can carry nothing out.

And having food and raiment let us be therewith content.

But they that will be rich fall into temptation and a snare, and into many foolish and hurtful lusts, which drown men in destruction and perdition.

For the love of money is the root of all evil: which while some coveted after, they have erred from the faith, and pierced themselves through with many sorrows.

But thou, O man of God, flee these things; and follow after righteousness, godliness, faith, love, patience, meekness.

Fight the good fight of faith, lay hold on eternal life, whereunto thou art also called, and hast professed a good profession before many witnesses.

—*1 Timothy 6:6–12*

Let your conversation be without covetousness; and be content with such things as ye have: for he hath said, I will never leave thee, nor forsake thee.

So that we may boldly say, The Lord is my helper, and I will not fear what man shall do unto me.

Remember them which have the rule over you, who have spoken unto you the word of God: whose faith follow, considering the end of their conversation.

—*Hebrews 13:5–7*

Go to now, ye rich men, weep and howl for your miseries that shall come upon you.

Your riches are corrupted, and your garments are motheaten.

Your gold and silver is cankered; and the rust of them shall be a witness against you, and shall eat your flesh as it were fire. Ye have heaped treasure together for the last days.

Behold, the hire of the labourers who have reaped down your fields, which is of you kept back by fraud, crieth: and the cries of them which have reaped are entered into the ears of the Lord of sabaoth.

Ye have lived in pleasure on the earth, and been wanton; ye have nourished your hearts, as in a day of slaughter.

Ye have condemned and killed the just; and he doth not resist you.

—James 5:1–6

❤ *Watch Out for the Wrong Motives and Goals*

Trust in the LORD, and do good; so shalt thou dwell in the land, and verily thou shalt be fed.

Delight thyself also in the LORD; and he shall give thee the desires of thine heart.

Commit thy way unto the LORD; trust also in him; and he shall bring it to pass.

And he shall bring forth thy righteousness as the light, and thy judgment as the noonday.

Rest in the LORD, and wait patiently for him: fret not thyself because of him who prospereth in his way, because of the man who bringeth wicked devices to pass. . . .

I have seen the wicked in great power, and spreading himself like a green bay tree.

—*Psalm 37:3–7, 35*

Wherefore do the wicked live, become old, yea, are mighty in power?

—*Job 21:7*

Moreover I will take from them the voice of mirth, and the voice of gladness, the voice of the bridegroom, and the voice of the bride, the sound of the millstones, and the light of the candle.

And this whole land shall be a desolation, and an astonishment; and these nations shall serve the king of Babylon seventy years.

—*Jeremiah 25:10–11*

❤ *Look Forward to Your Future with Him!*

For now we see through a glass, darkly; but then face to face: now I know in part; but then shall I know even as also I am known.

And now abideth faith, hope, charity, these three; but the greatest of these is charity.

—1 Corinthians 13:12–13

It is a faithful saying: For if we be dead with him, we shall also live with him:

If we suffer, we shall also reign with him: if we deny him, he also will deny us:

If we believe not, yet he abideth faithful: he cannot deny himself.

—2 Timothy 2:11–13

Let not your heart be troubled: ye believe in God, believe also in me.

In my Father's house are many mansions: if it were not so, I would have told you. I go to prepare a place for you.

And if I go and prepare a place for you, I will come again, and receive you unto myself; that where I am, there ye may be also.

And whither I go ye know, and the way ye know.

—John 14:1–4

There remaineth therefore a rest to the people of God.

—Hebrews 4:9

And I heard a voice from heaven saying unto me, Write, Blessed are the dead which die in the Lord from henceforth: Yea, saith the Spirit, that they may rest from their labours; and their works do follow them.

—Revelation 14:13

And I saw a new heaven and a new earth: for the first heaven and the first earth were passed away; and there was no more sea.

And I John saw the holy city, new Jerusalem, coming down from God out of heaven, prepared as a bride adorned for her husband.

And I heard a great voice out of heaven saying, Behold, the tabernacle of God is with men, and he will dwell with them, and they shall be his people, and God himself shall be with them, and be their God.

And God shall wipe away all tears from their eyes; and there shall be no more death, neither sorrow, nor crying, neither shall there be any more pain: for the former things are passed away.

And he that sat upon the throne said, Behold, I make all things new. And he said unto me, Write: for these words are true and faithful.

—*Revelation 21:1–5*

Six

Handling Conflict Wisely

It is possible to fight fair, but it takes quite a bit of flexibility and substantial doses of self-control. Biblical characters offer plenty of examples of both the right way and the wrong way to go about it. Take heed!

105

How Do You Handle Your Conflicts?

If I see conflict as natural, neutral, normal, I may be able to see the difficulties we experience as tension in relationships and honest differences in perspective that can be worked through by caring about each other and each confronting the other with truth expressed by love.

—David Augsburger[1]

Now I beseech you, brethren, by the name of our Lord Jesus Christ, that ye all speak the same thing, and that there be no divisions among you; but that ye be perfectly joined together in the same mind and in the same judgment.

—1 Corinthians 1:10

Lot also, which went with Abram, had flocks, and herds, and tents.

And the land was not able to bear them, that they might dwell together: for their substance was great, so that they could not dwell together.

And there was a strife between the herdmen of Abram's cattle and the herdmen of

Lot's cattle: and the Canaanite and the Perizzite dwelled then in the land.

And Abram said unto Lot, Let there be no strife, I pray thee, between me and thee, and between my herdmen and thy herdmen; for we be brethren.

Is not the whole land before thee? separate thyself, I pray thee, from me: if thou wilt take the left hand, then I will go to the right; or if thou depart to the right hand, then I will go to the left.

And Lot lifted up his eyes, and beheld all the plain of Jordan, that it was well watered every where, before the LORD destroyed Sodom and Gomorrah, even as the garden of the LORD, like the land of Egypt, as thou comest unto Zoar.

Then Lot chose him all the plain of Jordan; and Lot journeyed east: and they separated themselves the one from the other.

Abram dwelled in the land of Canaan, and Lot dwelled in the cities of the plain, and pitched his tent toward Sodom.

—*Genesis 13:5–12*

Think not that I am come to send peace on earth: I came not to send peace, but a sword.

For I am come to set a man at variance against his father, and the daughter against her mother, and the daughter in law against her mother in law.

And a man's foes shall be they of his own household.

He that loveth father or mother more than me is not worthy of me: and he that loveth son or daughter more than me is not worthy of me.

And he that taketh not his cross, and followeth after me, is not worthy of me.

He that findeth his life shall lose it: and he that loseth his life for my sake shall find it.

—*Matthew 10:34–39*

Again, think ye that we excuse ourselves unto you? we speak before God in Christ: but we do all things, dearly beloved, for your edifying.

For I fear, lest, when I come, I shall not find you such as I would, and that I shall be found unto you such as ye would not: lest there be debates, envyings, wraths, strifes, backbitings, whisperings, swellings, tumults:

—*2 Corinthians 12:19–20*

Finally, be ye all of one mind, having compassion one of another, love as brethren, be pitiful, be courteous.

—1 Peter 3:8

♥ When You're Frustrated . . .

My soul is weary of my life; I will leave my complaint upon myself; I will speak in the bitterness of my soul.

I will say unto God, Do not condemn me; shew me wherefore thou contendest with me.

Is it good unto thee that thou shouldest oppress, that thou shouldest despise the work of thine hands, and shine upon the counsel of the wicked?

Hast thou eyes of flesh? or seest thou as man seeth?

Are thy days as the days of man? are thy years as man's days,

That thou enquirest after mine iniquity, and searchest after my sin?

Thou knowest that I am not wicked; and there is none that can deliver out of thine hand.

Thine hands have made me and fashioned me together round about; yet thou dost destroy me.

Remember, I beseech thee, that thou hast made me as the clay; and wilt thou bring me into dust again?

—Job 10:1–9

I will lift up mine eyes unto the hills, from whence cometh my help.

My help cometh from the LORD, which made heaven and earth.

He will not suffer thy foot to be moved: he that keepeth thee will not slumber.

Behold, he that keepeth Israel shall neither slumber nor sleep.

The LORD is thy keeper: the LORD is thy shade upon thy right hand.

The sun shall not smite thee by day, nor the moon by night.

The LORD shall preserve thee from all evil: he shall preserve thy soul.

The LORD shall preserve thy going out and thy coming in from this time forth, and even for evermore.

—Psalm 121

❤ *When You're Angry...*

But I say unto you, That whosoever is angry with his brother without a cause shall be in danger of the judgment: and whosoever shall say to his brother, Raca, shall be in danger of the council: but whosoever shall say, Thou fool, shall be in danger of hell fire.

—Matthew 5:22

Be ye angry, and sin not: let not the sun go down upon your wrath.

—Ephesians 4:26

❤ *When You Feel Bitter...*

My soul is weary of my life; I will leave my complaint upon myself; I will speak in the bitterness of my soul.

—Job 10:1

Thou hast neither part nor lot in this matter: for thy heart is not right in the sight of God.

Repent therefore of this thy wickedness, and pray God, if perhaps the thought of thine heart may be forgiven thee.

For I perceive that thou art in the gall of bitterness, and in the bond of iniquity.

—*Acts 8:21–23*

Let all bitterness, and wrath, and anger, and clamour, and evil speaking, be put away from you, with all malice.

—*Ephesians 4:31*

Looking diligently lest any man fail of the grace of God; lest any root of bitterness springing up trouble you, and thereby many be defiled.

—*Hebrews 12:15*

Can You Exercise Humility?

O Father, give us the humility which
Realizes its ignorance,
Admits its ignorance,
Recognizes its need,
Welcomes advice,
Accepts rebuke.
Help us always
To praise rather than to criticize,
To sympathize rather than to condemn.
To encourage rather than to discourage,
To build rather than to destroy,
And to think of people at their best
rather than at their worst.
This we ask for thy name's sake.

—William Barclay

I beseech Euodias, and beseech Syntyche, that they be of the same mind in the Lord.

And I intreat thee also, true yokefellow, help those women which laboured with me in the gospel, with Clement also, and with other my fellowlabourers, whose names are in the book of life.

—Philippians 4:2–3

Surely he scorneth the scorners: but he giveth grace unto the lowly.

—Proverbs 3:34

The fear of the LORD is the instruction of wisdom; and before honour is humility.

—Proverbs 15:33

By humility and the fear of the LORD are riches, and honour, and life.

—Proverbs 22:4

But I say unto you, That ye resist not evil: but whosoever shall smite thee on thy right cheek, turn to him the other also.

—Matthew 5:39

For whosoever exalteth himself shall be abased; and he that humbleth himself shall be exalted.

—Luke 14:11

In those days came John the Baptist, preaching in the wilderness of Judaea,

And saying, Repent ye: for the kingdom of heaven is at hand.

For this is he that was spoken of by the prophet Esaias, saying, The voice of one crying in the wilderness, Prepare ye the way of the Lord, make his paths straight.

And the same John had his raiment of camel's hair, and a leathern girdle about his loins; and his meat was locusts and wild honey. . . .

I indeed baptize you with water unto repentance: but he that cometh after me is mightier than I, whose shoes I am not worthy to bear: he shall baptize you with the Holy Ghost, and with fire.

—*Matthew 3:1–4, 11*

Whosoever therefore shall confess me before men, him will I confess also before my Father which is in heaven.

But whosoever shall deny me before men, him will I also deny before my Father which is in heaven.

—*Matthew 10:32–33*

Ye adulterers and adulteresses, know ye not that the friendship of the world is enmity with God? whosoever therefore will be a friend of the world is the enemy of God.

Do ye think that the scripture saith in vain, The spirit that dwelleth in us lusteth to envy?

But he giveth more grace. Wherefore he saith, God resisteth the proud, but giveth grace unto the humble.

—*James 4:4–6*

Humble yourselves therefore under the mighty hand of God, that he may exalt you in due time.

—*1 Peter 5:6*

Will You Seek Contentment in This Situation?

Whatever comes, let's be content withall:
Among God's blessings there is not one small.
—*Robert Herrick*

Godliness with contentment is great gain.

For we brought nothing into this world, and it is certain we can carry nothing out.

And having food and raiment let us be therewith content.

—1 Timothy 6:6–8

And the king said unto Barzillai, Come thou over with me, and I will feed thee with me in Jerusalem.

And Barzillai said unto the king, How long have I to live, that I should go up with the king unto Jerusalem?

I am this day fourscore years old: and can I discern between good and evil? can thy servant taste what I eat or what I drink? can I hear any more the voice of singing men and singing women? wherefore then should thy servant be yet a burden unto my lord the king?

Thy servant will go a little way over Jordan with the king: and why should the king recompense it me with such a reward?

Let thy servant, I pray thee, turn back again, that I may die in mine own city, and be buried by the grave of my father and of my mother. But behold thy servant Chimham; let him go over with my lord the king; and do to him what shall seem good unto thee.

—2 Samuel 19:33–37

For a day in thy courts is better than a thousand. I had rather be a doorkeeper in the house of my God, than to dwell in the tents of wickedness.

For the LORD God is a sun and shield: the LORD will give grace and glory: no good thing will he withhold from them that walk uprightly.

O LORD of hosts, blessed is the man that trusteth in thee.

—Psalm 84:10–12

Two things have I required of thee; deny me them not before I die:

Remove far from me vanity and lies: give me neither poverty nor riches; feed me with food convenient for me:

Lest I be full, and deny thee, and say, Who is the LORD? or lest I be poor, and steal, and take the name of my God in vain.

—Proverbs 30:7–9

I know that there is no good in them, but for a man to rejoice, and to do good in his life.

And also that every man should eat and drink, and enjoy the good of all his labour, it is the gift of God.

—*Ecclesiastes 3:12–13*

Behold that which I have seen: it is good and comely for one to eat and to drink, and to enjoy the good of all his labour that he taketh under the sun all the days of his life, which God giveth him: for it is his portion.

Every man also to whom God hath given riches and wealth, and hath given him power to eat thereof, and to take his portion, and to rejoice in his labour; this is the gift of God.

For he shall not much remember the days of his life; because God answereth him in the joy of his heart.

—*Ecclesiastes 5:18–20*

All the labour of man is for his mouth, and yet the appetite is not filled.

For what hath the wise more than the fool? what hath the poor, that knoweth to walk before the living?

Better is the sight of the eyes than the wandering of the desire: this is also vanity and vexation of spirit.

—Ecclesiastes 6:7–9

Not that I speak in respect of want: for I have learned, in whatsoever state I am, therewith to be content.

I know both how to be abased, and I know how to abound: every where and in all things I am instructed both to be full and to be hungry, both to abound and to suffer need.

I can do all things through Christ which strengtheneth me.

—Philippians 4:11–13

Let your conversation be without covetousness; and be content with such things as ye have: for he hath said, I will never leave thee, nor forsake thee.

—Hebrews 13:5

Will You Let God's Peace Comfort You?

Resign every forbidden joy; restrain every wish that is not referred to God's will; banish all eager desires, all anxiety. Desire only the will of God; seek him alone and supremely, and you will find peace.

—Francois Fenelon

Thou shalt make thy prayer unto him, and he shall hear thee, and thou shalt pay thy vows.

Thou shalt also decree a thing, and it shall be established unto thee: and the light shall shine upon thy ways.

When men are cast down, then thou shalt say, There is lifting up; and he shall save the humble person.

He shall deliver the island of the innocent: and it is delivered by the pureness of thine hands.

—Job 22:27–30

Dominion and fear are with him, he maketh peace in his high places.

Is there any number of his armies? and upon whom doth not his light arise?

How then can man be justified with God? or how can he be clean that is born of a woman?

Behold even to the moon, and it shineth not; yea, the stars are not pure in his sight.

How much less man, that is a worm? and the son of man, which is a worm?

—*Job 25:2–6*

What man is he that feareth the LORD? him shall he teach in the way that he shall choose.

His soul shall dwell at ease; and his seed shall inherit the earth.

—*Psalm 25:12–13*

And he will destroy in this mountain the face of the covering cast over all people, and the vail that is spread over all nations.

He will swallow up death in victory; and the Lord GOD will wipe away tears from off all faces; and the rebuke of his people shall he take away from off all the earth: for the LORD hath spoken it.

—Isaiah 25:7–8

The righteous perisheth, and no man layeth it to heart: and merciful men are taken away, none considering that the righteous is taken away from the evil to come.

He shall enter into peace: they shall rest in their beds, each one walking in his uprightness. . . .

I create the fruit of the lips; Peace, peace to him that is far off, and to him that is near, saith the LORD; and I will heal him.

—Isaiah 57:1–2, 19

Now the God of hope fill you with all joy and peace in believing, that ye may abound in hope, through the power of the Holy Ghost. . . .

Now the God of peace be with you all. Amen.

—Romans 15:13, 33

And the peace of God, which passeth all understanding, shall keep your hearts and minds through Christ Jesus.

Finally, brethren, whatsoever things are true, whatsoever things are honest, whatsoever things are just, whatsoever things are pure, whatsoever things are lovely, whatsoever things are of good report; if there be any virtue, and if there be any praise, think on these things.

Those things, which ye have both learned, and received, and heard, and seen in me, do: and the God of peace shall be with you.

—*Philippians 4:7–9*

Seven

Dealing with Finances and Juggling Careers

It's not easy to make ends meet in today's family, whether we have children or not. And as busy as we are, we couples can become "ships passing in the night." What can we do when money and career concerns begin to consume all our thoughts, dictating the bulk of our daily activities? Somehow we've got to regain our peace of mind. God's Word offers help . . .

125

Feeling Worried about Money?

Riches are the pettiest and least worthy gifts which God can give a man. What are they to God's Word, to bodily gifts, such as beauty and health; or to the gifts of the mind, such as understanding, skill, wisdom?

Yet men toil for them day and night, and take not rest. Therefore God commonly gives riches to foolish people to whom he gives nothing else.

—Martin Luther

My bowels boiled, and rested not: the days of affliction prevented me.

—*Job 30:27*

I am feeble and sore broken: I have roared by reason of the disquietness of my heart.

—*Psalm 38:8*

Be careful for nothing; but in every thing by prayer and supplication with thanksgiving let your requests be made known unto God.

And the peace of God, which passeth all understanding, shall keep your hearts and minds through Christ Jesus. . . .

Not that I speak in respect of want: for I have learned, in whatsoever state I am, therewith to be content.

I know both how to be abased, and I know how to abound: every where and in all things I am instructed both to be full and to be hungry, both to abound and to suffer need.

I can do all things through Christ which strengtheneth me.

—*Philippians 4:6–7, 11–13*

❤ *Practice Good Stewardship*

The earth is the LORD's, and the fulness thereof; the world, and they that dwell therein.

For he hath founded it upon the seas, and established it upon the floods.

—*Psalm 24:1–2*

What? know ye not that your body is the temple of the Holy Ghost which is in you, which ye have of God, and ye are not your own?

For ye are bought with a price: therefore glorify God in your body, and in your spirit, which are God's.

—1 Corinthians 6:19–20

For I mean not that other men be eased, and ye burdened:

But by an equality, that now at this time your abundance may be a supply for their want, that their abundance also may be a supply for your want: that there may be equality:

As it is written, He that had gathered much had nothing over; and he that had gathered little had no lack.

—2 Corinthians 8:13–15

And when James, Cephas, and John, who seemed to be pillars, perceived the grace that was given unto me, they gave to me and Barnabas the right hands of fellowship; that we should go unto the heathen, and they unto the circumcision.

Only they would that we should remember the poor; the same which I also was forward to do.

—Galatians 2:9–10

As every man hath received the gift, even so minister the same one to another, as good stewards of the manifold grace of God.

If any man speak, let him speak as the oracles of God; if any man minister, let him do it as of the ability which God giveth: that God in all things may be glorified through Jesus Christ, to whom be praise and dominion for ever and ever. Amen.

—*1 Peter 4:10–11*

♥ *Use Possessions Wisely and Frugally*

And he gathered up all the food of the seven years, which were in the land of Egypt, and laid up the food in the cities: the food of the field, which was round about every city, laid he up in the same.

And Joseph gathered corn as the sand of the sea, very much, until he left numbering; for it was without number.

And unto Joseph were born two sons before the years of famine came, which Asenath the daughter of Poti-pherah priest of On bare unto him.

129

And Joseph called the name of the firstborn Manasseh: For God, said he, hath made me forget all my toil, and all my father's house.

And the name of the second called he Ephraim: For God hath caused me to be fruitful in the land of my affliction.

And the seven years of plenteousness, that was in the land of Egypt, were ended.

And the seven years of dearth began to come, according as Joseph had said: and the dearth was in all lands; but in all the land of Egypt there was bread.

—*Genesis 41:48–53*

A good man leaveth an inheritance to his children's children: and the wealth of the sinner is laid up for the just.

—*Proverbs 13:22*

He that loveth pleasure shall be a poor man: he that loveth wine and oil shall not be rich.

The wicked shall be a ransom for the righteous, and the transgressor for the upright.

It is better to dwell in the wilderness, than with a contentious and an angry woman.

There is treasure to be desired and oil in the dwelling of the wise; but a foolish man spendeth it up.

He that followeth after righteousness and mercy findeth life, righteousness, and honour.

—*Proverbs 21:17–21*

Be not among winebibbers; among riotous eaters of flesh:

For the drunkard and the glutton shall come to poverty: and drowsiness shall clothe a man with rags.

—*Proverbs 23:20–21*

And they did all eat, and were filled: and they took up of the broken meat that was left seven baskets full.

—*Matthew 15:37*

Jesus entered and passed through Jericho.

And, behold, there was a man named Zacchaeus, which was the chief among the publicans, and he was rich.

And he sought to see Jesus who he was; and could not for the press, because he was little of stature.

And he ran before, and climbed up into a sycomore tree to see him: for he was to pass that way.

And when Jesus came to the place, he looked up, and saw him, and said unto him, Zacchaeus, make haste, and come down; for to day I must abide at thy house.

And he made haste, and came down, and received him joyfully.

And when they saw it, they all murmured, saying, That he was gone to be guest with a man that is a sinner.

And Zacchaeus stood, and said unto the Lord; Behold, Lord, the half of my goods I give to the poor; and if I have taken any thing from any man by false accusation, I restore him fourfold.

And Jesus said unto him, This day is salvation come to this house, forsomuch as he also is a son of Abraham.

For the Son of man is come to seek and to save that which was lost.

—*Luke 19:1–10*

And when James, Cephas, and John, who seemed to be pillars, perceived the grace that was given unto me, they gave to me and Barnabas the right hands of fellowship; that we should go unto the heathen, and they unto the circumcision.

Only they would that we should remember the poor; the same which I also was forward to do.

—*Galatians 2:9–10*

Feeling Like a Failure at Work?

Many workers in the modern marketplace feel increasingly bored with their jobs and with life. This is the subtext of all the glitzy beer, hamburger, and travel commercials that show hardworking laborers building America and solving its problems. They portray the work place not as it is but as we wish it could be—an engrossing, challenging, even uplifting human drama in which each of us performs our strategic role and fulfills a personal mission. Instead, for many work is "just a job." Its value begins and ends with a paycheck.

—*Doug Sherman and William Hendricks*[1]

I will extol thee, O LORD; for thou hast lifted me up, and hast not made my foes to rejoice over me.

O LORD my God, I cried unto thee, and thou hast healed me.

O LORD, thou hast brought up my soul from the grave: thou hast kept me alive, that I should not go down to the pit.

Sing unto the LORD, O ye saints of his, and give thanks at the remembrance of his holiness.

For his anger endureth but a moment; in his favour is life: weeping may endure for a night, but joy cometh in the morning.

—*Psalm 30:1–5*

The LORD is nigh unto them that are of a broken heart; and saveth such as be of a contrite spirit.

Psalm 34:18

Commit thy works unto the LORD, and thy thoughts shall be established.

—*Proverbs 16:3*

But none of these things move me, neither count I my life dear unto myself, so that I might finish my course with joy, and the ministry, which I have received of the Lord Jesus, to testify the gospel of the grace of God.

—*Acts 20:24*

But we have this treasure in earthen vessels, that the excellency of the power may be of God, and not of us.

We are troubled on every side, yet not distressed; we are perplexed, but not in despair;

Persecuted, but not forsaken; cast down, but not destroyed;

Always bearing about in the body the dying of the Lord Jesus, that the life also of Jesus might be made manifest in our body.

For we which live are alway delivered unto death for Jesus' sake, that the life also of Jesus might be made manifest in our mortal flesh.

—2 Corinthians 4:7–11

❤ *Welcome Hard Work*

Go to the ant, thou sluggard; consider her ways, and be wise:

Which having no guide, overseer, or ruler,

Provideth her meat in the summer, and gathereth her food in the harvest.

How long wilt thou sleep, O sluggard? when wilt thou arise out of thy sleep?

Yet a little sleep, a little slumber, a little folding of the hands to sleep:

So shall thy poverty come as one that travelleth, and thy want as an armed man.

—*Proverbs 6:6–11*

He that tilleth his land shall be satisfied with bread: but he that followeth vain persons is void of understanding. . . .

The hand of the diligent shall bear rule: but the slothful shall be under tribute.

Heaviness in the heart of man maketh it stoop: but a good word maketh it glad.

The righteous is more excellent than his neighbour: but the way of the wicked seduceth them.

The slothful man roasteth not that which he took in hunting: but the substance of a diligent man is precious.

—*Proverbs 12:11, 24–27*

Be thou diligent to know the state of thy flocks, and look well to thy herds.

For riches are not for ever: and doth the crown endure to every generation?

The hay appeareth, and the tender grass sheweth itself, and herbs of the mountains are gathered.

The lambs are for thy clothing, and the goats are the price of the field.

And thou shalt have goats' milk enough for thy food, for the food of thy household, and for the maintenance for thy maidens.

—Proverbs 27:23–27

The ants are a people not strong, yet they prepare their meat in the summer;

The conies are but a feeble folk, yet make they their houses in the rocks;

The locusts have no king, yet go they forth all of them by bands;

The spider taketh hold with her hands, and is in kings' palaces.

—Proverbs 30:25–28

I have coveted no man's silver, or gold, or apparel.

Yea, ye yourselves know, that these hands have ministered unto my necessities, and to them that were with me.

—Acts 20:33–34

Know ye not that they which run in a race run all, but one receiveth the prize? So run, that ye may obtain.

And every man that striveth for the mastery is temperate in all things. Now they do it to obtain a corruptible crown; but we an incorruptible.

I therefore so run, not as uncertainly; so fight I, not as one that beateth the air:

But I keep under my body, and bring it into subjection: lest that by any means, when I have preached to others, I myself should be a castaway.

—*1 Corinthians 9:24–27*

And that ye study to be quiet, and to do your own business, and to work with your own hands, as we commanded you;

That ye may walk honestly toward them that are without, and that ye may have lack of nothing.

—*1 Thessalonians 4:11–12*

For even when we were with you, this we commanded you, that if any would not work, neither should he eat.

For we hear that there are some which walk among you disorderly, working not at all, but are busybodies.

Now them that are such we command and exhort by our Lord Jesus Christ, that with quietness they work, and eat their own bread.

—*2 Thessalonians 3:10–12*

❤ *Avoid Untrustworthy Actions at Work*

Hear another parable: There was a certain householder, which planted a vineyard, and hedged it round about, and digged a winepress in it, and built a tower, and let it out to husbandmen, and went into a far country:

And when the time of the fruit drew near, he sent his servants to the husbandmen, that they might receive the fruits of it.

And the husbandmen took his servants, and beat one, and killed another, and stoned another.

Again, he sent other servants more than the first: and they did unto them likewise.

But last of all he sent unto them his son, saying, They will reverence my son.

But when the husbandmen saw the son, they said among themselves, This is the heir;

come, let us kill him, and let us seize on his inheritance.

And they caught him, and cast him out of the vineyard, and slew him.

When the lord therefore of the vineyard cometh, what will he do unto those husbandmen?

They say unto him, He will miserably destroy those wicked men, and will let out his vineyard unto other husbandmen, which shall render him the fruits in their seasons.

—*Matthew 21:33–41*

Art thou called being a servant? care not for it: but if thou mayest be made free, use it rather.

For he that is called in the Lord, being a servant, is the Lord's freeman: likewise also he that is called, being free, is Christ's servant.

Ye are bought with a price; be not ye the servants of men.

—*1 Corinthians 7:21–23*

❤ *Rest in God's Peace*

Six days thou shalt do thy work, and on the seventh day thou shalt rest: that thine ox and thine ass may rest, and the son of thy handmaid, and the stranger, may be refreshed.

—Exodus 23:12

Thou wilt keep him in perfect peace, whose mind is stayed on thee: because he trusteth in thee.

—Isaiah 26:3

For he shall be as a tree planted by the waters, and that spreadeth out her roots by the river, and shall not see when heat cometh, but her leaf shall be green; and shall not be careful in the year of drought, neither shall cease from yielding fruit.

—Jeremiah 17:8

These things I have spoken unto you, that in me ye might have peace. In the world ye shall have tribulation: but be of good cheer; I have overcome the world.

—John 16:33

But he that prophesieth speaketh unto men to edification, and exhortation, and comfort.

—1 Corinthians 14:3

For he is our peace, who hath made both one, and hath broken down the middle wall of partition between us;

Having abolished in his flesh the enmity, even the law of commandments contained in ordinances; for to make in himself of twain one new man, so making peace;

And that he might reconcile both unto God in one body by the cross, having slain the enmity thereby:

And came and preached peace to you which were afar off, and to them that were nigh.

—Ephesians 2:14–17

And the peace of God, which passeth all understanding, shall keep your hearts and minds through Christ Jesus.

—Philippians 4:7

Now the Lord of peace himself give you peace always by all means. The Lord be with you all.

—2 Thessalonians 3:16

Maintaining Personal Devotion

Why do we so often fail to make time for what is truly most important to us: our relationship with God? Perhaps it is the sense that other things—the myriad concerns that press upon us right now—seem much more real.

Yet, in reality, God dwells at the center of our lives always, whether we acknowledge His presence or not. He is simply waiting for us to turn

*our attention to Him. It's a small shift in per-
spective, with awesome spiritual benefit!
He is there, waiting.*

Get to Know Your God!

*The world is too much with us;
late and soon,
Getting and spending, we lay
waste our powers:
Little we see in Nature that is ours;
We have given our hearts away,
a sordid boon!*

—William Wordsworth

Then Paul stood in the midst of Mars' hill, and said, Ye men of Athens, I perceive that in all things ye are too superstitious.

For as I passed by, and beheld your devotions, I found an altar with this inscription, TO THE UNKNOWN GOD. Whom therefore ye ignorantly worship, him declare I unto you.

God that made the world and all things therein, seeing that he is Lord of heaven and earth, dwelleth not in temples made with hands;

Neither is worshipped with men's hands, as though he needed any thing, seeing he giveth to all life, and breath, and all things;

And hath made of one blood all nations of men for to dwell on all the face of the earth, and hath determined the times before appointed, and the bounds of their habitation;

That they should seek the Lord, if haply they might feel after him, and find him, though he be not far from every one of us.

—*Acts 17:22–27*

Be still, and know that I am God:
I will be exalted among the heathen,
I will be exalted in the earth.

—*Psalm 46:10*

146

❤ *Seek Him in Regular Times of Silence*

Stand in awe, and sin not: commune with your own heart upon your bed, and be still. Selah.

—Psalm 4:4

Better is an handful with quietness, than both the hands full with travail and vexation of spirit.

—Ecclesiastes 4:6

Let the words of my mouth, and the meditation of my heart, be acceptable in thy sight, O LORD, my strength, and my redeemer.

—Psalm 19:14

I said, I will take heed to my ways, that I sin not with my tongue: I will keep my mouth with a bridle, while the wicked is before me.

I was dumb with silence, I held my peace, even from good; and my sorrow was stirred.

My heart was hot within me, while I was musing the fire burned: then spake I with my tongue.

—Psalm 39:1–3

Hear this, all ye people; give ear, all ye inhabitants of the world:

Both low and high, rich and poor, together.

My mouth shall speak of wisdom; and the meditation of my heart shall be of understanding.

—Psalm 49:1–3

My soul shall be satisfied as with marrow and fatness; and my mouth shall praise thee with joyful lips:

When I remember thee upon my bed, and meditate on thee in the night watches.

—Psalm 63:5–6

And I said, This is my infirmity: but I will remember the years of the right hand of the most High.

I will remember the works of the LORD: surely I will remember thy wonders of old.

I will meditate also of all thy work, and talk of thy doings.

—Psalm 77:10–12

How precious also are thy thoughts unto me, O God! how great is the sum of them!

If I should count them, they are more in number than the sand: when I awake, I am still with thee.

—*Psalm 139:17–18*

♥ *Listen to His Word*

Thy word have I hid in mine heart, that I might not sin against thee.

I will delight myself in thy statutes: I will not forget thy word.

So shall I have wherewith to answer him that reproacheth me: for I trust in thy word.

This is my comfort in my affliction: for thy word hath quickened me.

—*Psalm 119:11, 16, 42, 50*

All scripture is given by inspiration of God, and is profitable for doctrine, for reproof, for correction, for instruction in righteousness:

That the man of God may be perfect, throughly furnished unto all good works.

—*2 Timothy 3:16–17*

For the word of God is quick, and powerful, and sharper than any twoedged sword, piercing even to the dividing asunder of soul and spirit, and of the joints and marrow, and is a discerner of the thoughts and intents of the heart.

Neither is there any creature that is not manifest in his sight: but all things are naked and opened unto the eyes of him with whom we have to do.

—*Hebrews 4:12–13*

💗 *Determine to Obey His Will*

Cause me to hear thy lovingkindness in the morning; for in thee do I trust: cause me to know the way wherein I should walk; for I lift up my soul unto thee.

—*Psalm 143:8*

Ye are the light of the world. A city that is set on an hill cannot be hid.

Neither do men light a candle, and put it under a bushel, but on a candlestick; and it giveth light unto all that are in the house.

150

Let your light so shine before men, that they may see your good works, and glorify your Father which is in heaven.

—Matthew 5:14–16

And now, Israel, what doth the LORD thy God require of thee, but to fear the LORD thy God, to walk in all his ways, and to love him, and to serve the LORD thy God with all thy heart and with all thy soul,

To keep the commandments of the LORD, and his statutes, which I command thee this day for thy good?

—Deuteronomy 10:12–13

Blessed are the undefiled in the way, who walk in the law of the LORD.

Blessed are they that keep his testimonies, and that seek him with the whole heart.

They also do no iniquity: they walk in his ways.

Thou hast commanded us to keep thy precepts diligently.

O that my ways were directed to keep thy statutes!

—Psalm 119:1–5

151

The night is far spent, the day is at hand: let us therefore cast off the works of darkness, and let us put on the armour of light.

Let us walk honestly, as in the day; not in rioting and drunkenness, not in chambering and wantonness, not in strife and envying.

But put ye on the Lord Jesus Christ, and make not provision for the flesh, to fulfil the lusts thereof.

—*Romans 13:12–14*

I, therefore, the prisoner of the Lord, beseech you that ye walk worthy of the vocation wherewith ye are called,

With all lowliness and meekness, with longsuffering, forbearing one another in love.

—*Ephesians 4:1–2*

Having your conversation honest among the Gentiles: that, whereas they speak against you as evildoers, they may by your good works, which they shall behold, glorify God in the day of visitation.

Submit yourselves to every ordinance of man for the Lord's sake: whether it be to the king, as supreme;

Or unto governors, as unto them that are sent by him for the punishment of evildoers, and for the praise of them that do well.

For so is the will of God, that with well doing ye may put to silence the ignorance of foolish men.

—*1 Peter 2:12–15*

❤ *Live Daily in God's Strength*

O God, thou art my God; early will I seek thee: my soul thirsteth for thee, my flesh longeth for thee in a dry and thirsty land, where no water is.

—*Psalm 63:1*

For by thee I have run through a troop: by my God have I leaped over a wall.

—*2 Samuel 22:30*

When thou goest, thy steps shall not be straitened; and when thou runnest, thou shalt not stumble.

—*Proverbs 4:12*

153

He giveth power to the faint; and to them that have no might he increaseth strength.

Even the youths shall faint and be weary, and the young men shall utterly fall:

But they that wait upon the LORD shall renew their strength; they shall mount up with wings as eagles; they shall run, and not be weary; and they shall walk, and not faint.

—Isaiah 40:29–31

Although the fig tree shall not blossom, neither shall fruit be in the vines; the labour of the olive shall fail, and the fields shall yield no meat; the flock shall be cut off from the fold, and there shall be no herd in the stalls:

Yet I will rejoice in the LORD, I will joy in the God of my salvation.

—Habakkuk 3:17–18

Ask, and it shall be given you; seek, and ye shall find; knock, and it shall be opened unto you.

—Matthew 7:7

I beseech you therefore, brethren, by the mercies of God, that ye present your bodies a living sacrifice, holy, acceptable unto God, which is your reasonable service.

—*Romans 12:1*

Develop Your Prayer Life

God hears no more than the heart speaks; and if the heart be dumb, God will certainly be deaf.

—*Thomas Brooks*

Thou shalt make thy prayer unto him, and he shall hear thee, and thou shalt pay thy vows.

Thou shalt also decree a thing, and it shall be established unto thee: and the light shall shine upon thy ways.

—*Job 22:27–28*

After this manner therefore pray ye: Our Father which art in heaven, Hallowed be thy name.

Thy kingdom come. Thy will be done in earth, as it is in heaven.

Give us this day our daily bread.

And forgive us our debts, as we forgive our debtors.

And lead us not into temptation, but deliver us from evil: For thine is the kingdom, and the power, and the glory, for ever. Amen.

—*Matthew 6:9–13*

Verily I say unto you, Whatsoever ye shall bind on earth shall be bound in heaven: and whatsoever ye shall loose on earth shall be loosed in heaven.

—*Matthew 18:18*

Be careful for nothing; but in every thing by prayer and supplication with thanksgiving let your requests be made known unto God.

—*Philippians 4:6*

Let us therefore come boldly unto the throne of grace, that we may obtain mercy, and find grace to help in time of need.

—*Hebrews 4:16*

Let us draw near with a true heart in full assurance of faith, having our hearts sprin-

156

kled from an evil conscience, and our bodies washed with pure water.

—*Hebrews 10:22*

But without faith it is impossible to please him: for he that cometh to God must believe that he is, and that he is a rewarder of them that diligently seek him.

—*Hebrews 11:6*

And whatsoever we ask, we receive of him, because we keep his commandments, and do those things that are pleasing in his sight.

—*1 John 3:22*

These things have I written unto you that believe on the name of the Son of God; that ye may know that ye have eternal life, and that ye may believe on the name of the Son of God.

And this is the confidence that we have in him, that, if we ask any thing according to his will, he heareth us:

And if we know that he hear us, whatsoever we ask, we know that we have the petitions that we desired of him.

—*1 John 5:13–15*

Strengthen Your Personal Witness

Fight the temptation to be bashful about the Christian faith. Avoid a bashful brand of Christian that tiptoes up to people and hesitantly suggests: "I may be wrong, but I'm afraid that if you do not repent after a fashion and receive Christ, so to speak, you might be damned, as it were."

—William A. Ward

This I say, brethren, the time is short.

—1 Corinthians 7:29

Also I say unto you, Whosoever shall confess me before men, him shall the Son of man also confess before the angels of God:

But he that denieth me before men shall be denied before the angels of God.

—Luke 12:8–9

No man, when he hath lighted a candle, covereth it with a vessel, or putteth it under a bed; but setteth it on a candlestick, that they which enter in may see the light. . . .

Now the man out of whom the devils were departed besought him that he might be with him: but Jesus sent him away, saying,

Return to thine own house, and shew how great things God hath done unto thee. And he went his way, and published throughout the whole city how great things Jesus had done unto him.

—*Luke 8:16, 38–39*

For I will not dare to speak of any of those things which Christ hath not wrought by me, to make the Gentiles obedient, by word and deed,

Through mighty signs and wonders, by the power of the Spirit of God; so that from Jerusalem, and round about unto Illyricum, I have fully preached the gospel of Christ.

Yea, so have I strived to preach the gospel, not where Christ was named, lest I should build upon another man's foundation:

But as it is written, To whom he was not spoken of, they shall see: and they that have not heard shall understand.

—*Romans 15:18–21*

Keep Growing in Faith

*The Christian ideal has not been tried
and found wanting;
it has been found difficult and left untried.*
—G. K. Chesterton

For with God nothing shall be impossible.
—*Luke 1:37*

Now faith is the substance of things hoped for, the evidence of things not seen.
—*Hebrews 11:1*

For whatsoever is born of God overcometh the world: and this is the victory that overcometh the world, even our faith.

Who is he that overcometh the world, but he that believeth that Jesus is the Son of God?

This is he that came by water and blood, even Jesus Christ; not by water only, but by water and blood. And it is the Spirit that beareth witness, because the Spirit is truth.

For there are three that bear record in heaven, the Father, the Word, and the Holy Ghost: and these three are one.

And there are three that bear witness in earth, the spirit, and the water, and the blood: and these three agree in one.

If we receive the witness of men, the witness of God is greater: for this is the witness of God which he hath testified of his Son.

He that believeth on the Son of God hath the witness in himself: he that believeth not God hath made him a liar; because he believeth not the record that God gave of his Son.

And this is the record, that God hath given to us eternal life, and this life is in his Son.

He that hath the Son hath life; and he that hath not the Son of God hath not life.

These things have I written unto you that believe on the name of the Son of God; that ye may know that ye have eternal life, and that ye may believe on the name of the Son of God.

And this is the confidence that we have in him, that, if we ask any thing according to his will, he heareth us:

And if we know that he hear us, whatsoever we ask, we know that we have the petitions that we desired of him.

—*1 John 5:4–15*

Verily I say unto you, If ye have faith as a grain of mustard seed, ye shall say unto this mountain, Remove hence to yonder place; and it shall remove; and nothing shall be impossible unto you.

—*Matthew 17:20b*

— N i n e —

Surviving the Tough Times

Jesus said we shouldn't expect an easy time of it on earth. There will always be trials and tribulations. But we can expect the one thing we may forget in the midst of our suffering: His promise to be right there with us. Always.

Rely on God's Strength . . .

When you have no helpers, see all your helpers in God. When you have many helpers, see God

163

in all your helpers. When you have nothing but God, see all in God; when you have everything, see God in everything. Under all conditions, stay thy heart only on the Lord.

—*Charles Haddon Spurgeon*

And such trust have we through Christ to God-ward:

Not that we are sufficient of ourselves to think any thing as of ourselves; but our sufficiency is of God.

—*2 Corinthians 3:4–5*

My help cometh from the LORD, which made heaven and earth.

He will not suffer thy foot to be moved: he that keepeth thee will not slumber.

—*Psalm 121:2–3*

Seeing then that we have a great high priest, that is passed into the heavens, Jesus the Son of God, let us hold fast our profession.

For we have not an high priest which cannot be touched with the feeling of our infirmities; but was in all points tempted like as we are, yet without sin.

Let us therefore come boldly unto the throne of grace, that we may obtain mercy, and find grace to help in time of need.

—*Hebrews 4:14–16*

I can do all things through Christ which strengtheneth me.

—*Philippians 4:13*

❤ *When You're Afraid*

The LORD is my light and my salvation; whom shall I fear? the LORD is the strength of my life; of whom shall I be afraid?

When the wicked, even mine enemies and my foes, came upon me to eat up my flesh, they stumbled and fell.

Though an host should encamp against me, my heart shall not fear: though war should rise against me, in this will I be confident.

—*Psalm 27:1–3*

Therefore will not we fear, though the earth be removed, and though the mountains be carried into the midst of the sea.

Psalm 46:2

Hearken unto me, ye that know righteousness, the people in whose heart is my law; fear ye not the reproach of men, neither be ye afraid of their revilings.

—*Isaiah 51:7*

For God hath not given us the spirit of fear; but of power, and of love, and of a sound mind.

—*2 Timothy 1:7*

There is no fear in love; but perfect love casteth out fear: because fear hath torment. He that feareth is not made perfect in love.

—*1 John 4:18*

❤ *When You Feel Depressed*

Have mercy upon me, O LORD; for I am weak: O LORD, heal me; for my bones are vexed.

My soul is also sore vexed: but thou, O LORD, how long?

—*Psalm 6:2–3*

So I returned, and considered all the oppressions that are done under the sun: and behold the tears of such as were oppressed,

166

and they had no comforter; and on the side of their oppressors there was power; but they had no comforter.

Wherefore I praised the dead which are already dead more than the living which are yet alive.

—*Ecclesiastes 4:1–2*

He giveth power to the faint; and to them that have no might he increaseth strength.

Even the youths shall faint and be weary, and the young men shall utterly fall:

But they that wait upon the LORD shall renew their strength; they shall mount up with wings as eagles; they shall run, and not be weary; and they shall walk, and not faint.

—*Isaiah 40:29–31*

Come unto me, all ye that labour and are heavy laden, and I will give you rest.

Take my yoke upon you, and learn of me; for I am meek and lowly in heart: and ye shall find rest unto your souls.

For my yoke is easy, and my burden is light.

—*Matthew 11:28–30*

The apostles gathered themselves together unto Jesus, and told him all things, both what they had done, and what they had taught.

And he said unto them, Come ye yourselves apart into a desert place, and rest a while: for there were many coming and going, and they had no leisure so much as to eat.

And they departed into a desert place by ship privately.

—*Mark 6:30–32*

But God hath chosen the foolish things of the world to confound the wise; and God hath chosen the weak things of the world to confound the things which are mighty.

—*1 Corinthians 1:27*

For, when we were come into Macedonia, our flesh had no rest, but we were troubled on every side; without were fightings, within were fears.

Nevertheless God, that comforteth those that are cast down, comforted us by the coming of Titus;

And not by his coming only, but by the consolation wherewith he was comforted in you, when he told us your earnest desire, your mourning, your fervent mind toward me; so that I rejoiced the more.

—2 Corinthians 7:5–7

And let us not be weary in well doing: for in due season we shall reap, if we faint not.

—Galatians 6:9

❤ *When You're Stressed Out with Worry*

Now it came to pass on a certain day, that he went into a ship with his disciples: and he said unto them, Let us go over unto the other side of the lake. And they launched forth.

But as they sailed he fell asleep: and there came down a storm of wind on the lake; and they were filled with water, and were in jeopardy.

And they came to him, and awoke him, saying, Master, master, we perish. Then he arose, and rebuked the wind and the raging of the water: and they ceased, and there was a calm.

And he said unto them, Where is your faith? And they being afraid wondered, saying

169

one to another, What manner of man is this! for he commandeth even the winds and water, and they obey him.

—Luke 8:22–25

Peace I leave with you, my peace I give unto you: not as the world giveth, give I unto you. Let not your heart be troubled, neither let it be afraid.

—John 14:27

Now the Lord of peace himself give you peace always by all means. The Lord be with you all.

—2 Thessalonians 3:16

❤ *When You're Overcome with Doubts. . .*

Have not I commanded thee? Be strong and of a good courage; be not afraid, neither be thou dismayed: for the LORD thy God is with thee whithersoever thou goest.

—Joshua 1:9

Behold, I am the LORD, the God of all flesh: is there any thing too hard for me?

—Jeremiah 32:27

170

And, behold, a woman, which was diseased with an issue of blood twelve years, came behind him, and touched the hem of his garment:

For she said within herself, If I may but touch his garment, I shall be whole.

But Jesus turned him about, and when he saw her, he said, Daughter, be of good comfort; thy faith hath made thee whole. And the woman was made whole from that hour.

—*Matthew 9:20–22*

For with God nothing shall be impossible.

—*Luke 1:37*

We are troubled on every side, yet not distressed; we are perplexed, but not in despair;

Persecuted, but not forsaken; cast down, but not destroyed;

Always bearing about in the body the dying of the Lord Jesus, that the life also of Jesus might be made manifest in our body.

—*2 Corinthians 4:8–10*

For we walk by faith, not by sight.

—*2 Corinthians 5:7*

❤ *When You Feel Ashamed . . .*

Thou hast known my reproach, and my shame, and my dishonour: mine adversaries are all before thee.

—Psalm 69:19

Fear not; for thou shalt not be ashamed: neither be thou confounded; for thou shalt not be put to shame: for thou shalt forget the shame of thy youth, and shalt not remember the reproach of thy widowhood any more.

—Isaiah 54:4

For your shame ye shall have double; and for confusion they shall rejoice in their portion: therefore in their land they shall possess the double: everlasting joy shall be unto them.

—Isaiah 61:7

Ye shall eat in plenty, and be satisfied, and praise the name of the LORD your God, that hath dealt wondrously with you: and my people shall never be ashamed.

And ye shall know that I am in the midst of Israel, and that I am the LORD your God, and none else: and my people shall never be ashamed.

—*Joel 2:26–27*

As it is written, Behold, I lay in Sion a stumblingstone and rock of offence: and whosoever believeth on him shall not be ashamed.

—*Romans 9:33*

❤ *When You Feel Tempted . . .*

The LORD shall preserve thee from all evil: he shall preserve thy soul.

The LORD shall preserve thy going out and thy coming in from this time forth, and even for evermore.

—*Psalm 121:7–8*

Rejoice not against me, O mine enemy: when I fall, I shall arise; when I sit in darkness, the LORD shall be a light unto me.

—*Micah 7:8*

For the weapons of our warfare are not carnal, but mighty through God to the pulling down of strong holds.

—2 Corinthians 10:4

Put on the whole armour of God, that ye may be able to stand against the wiles of the devil.

For we wrestle not against flesh and blood, but against principalities, against powers, against the rulers of the darkness of this world, against spiritual wickedness in high places.

Wherefore take unto you the whole armour of God, that ye may be able to withstand in the evil day, and having done all, to stand.

Stand therefore, having your loins girt about with truth, and having on the breastplate of righteousness.

—Ephesians 6:11–14

But the Lord is faithful, who shall stablish you, and keep you from evil.

—2 Thessalonians 3:3

And the Lord shall deliver me from every evil work, and will preserve me unto his heavenly kingdom: to whom be glory for ever and ever. Amen.

—2 Timothy 4:18

Ye adulterers and adulteresses, know ye not that the friendship of the world is enmity with God? whosoever therefore will be a friend of the world is the enemy of God.

Submit yourselves therefore to God. Resist the devil, and he will flee from you.

Draw nigh to God, and he will draw nigh to you. Cleanse your hands, ye sinners; and purify your hearts, ye double minded.

—James 4:4, 7–8

The Lord knoweth how to deliver the godly out of temptations, and to reserve the unjust unto the day of judgment to be punished.

—2 Peter 2:9

Recall the Power of Christ . . .

Jesus! the name high over all,
In hell, or earth, or sky;
Angels and men before it fall,
And devils fear and fly.

—*Charles Wesley*

When my soul fainted within me I remembered the LORD: and my prayer came in unto thee.

—*Jonah 2:7a*

Who is the image of the invisible God, the firstborn of every creature:

For by him were all things created, that are in heaven, and that are in earth, visible and invisible, whether they be thrones, or dominions, or principalities, or powers: all things were created by him, and for him:

And he is before all things, and by him all things consist.

And he is the head of the body, the church: who is the beginning, the firstborn from the dead; that in all things he might have the preeminence.

For it pleased the Father that in him should all fulness dwell.

—*Colossians 1:15–19*

❤ *His Power Over Nature*

[Jesus] left them, and went out of the city into Bethany; and he lodged there.

Now in the morning as he returned into the city, he hungered.

And when he saw a fig tree in the way, he came to it, and found nothing thereon, but leaves only, and said unto it, Let no fruit grow on thee henceforward for ever. And presently the fig tree withered away.

And when the disciples saw it, they marvelled, saying, How soon is the fig tree withered away!

Jesus answered and said unto them, Verily I say unto you, If ye have faith, and doubt not, ye shall not only do this which is done to the fig tree, but also if ye shall say unto this mountain, Be thou removed, and be thou cast into the sea; it shall be done.

177

And all things, whatsoever ye shall ask in prayer, believing, ye shall receive.

—*Matthew 21:17–22*

The third day there was a marriage in Cana of Galilee; and the mother of Jesus was there:

And both Jesus was called, and his disciples, to the marriage.

And when they wanted wine, the mother of Jesus saith unto him, They have no wine.

Jesus saith unto her, Woman, what have I to do with thee? mine hour is not yet come.

His mother saith unto the servants, Whatsoever he saith unto you, do it.

And there were set there six waterpots of stone, after the manner of the purifying of the Jews, containing two or three firkins apiece.

Jesus saith unto them, Fill the waterpots with water. And they filled them up to the brim.

And he saith unto them, Draw out now, and bear unto the governor of the feast. And they bare it.

When the ruler of the feast had tasted the water that was made wine, and knew not whence it was: (but the servants which drew the water knew;) the governor of the feast called the bridegroom,

And saith unto him, Every man at the beginning doth set forth good wine; and when men have well drunk, then that which is worse: but thou hast kept the good wine until now.

This beginning of miracles did Jesus in Cana of Galilee, and manifested forth his glory; and his disciples believed on him.

—*John 2:1–11*

And when they were come to Capernaum, they that received tribute money came to Peter, and said, Doth not your master pay tribute?

He saith, Yes. And when he was come into the house, Jesus prevented him, saying, What thinkest thou, Simon? of whom do the kings of the earth take custom or tribute? of their own children, or of strangers?

Peter saith unto him, Of strangers. Jesus saith unto him, Then are the children free.

Notwithstanding, lest we should offend them, go thou to the sea, and cast an hook, and take up the fish that first cometh up; and when thou hast opened his mouth, thou shalt find a piece of money: that take, and give unto them for me and thee.

—*Matthew 17:24–27*

❤ *His Power Over Death Itself*

And it came to pass the day after, that [Jesus] went into a city called Nain; and many of his disciples went with him, and much people.

Now when he came nigh to the gate of the city, behold, there was a dead man carried out, the only son of his mother, and she was a widow: and much people of the city was with her.

And when the Lord saw her, he had compassion on her, and said unto her, Weep not.

And he came and touched the bier: and they that bare him stood still. And he said, Young man, I say unto thee, Arise.

And he that was dead sat up, and began to speak. And he delivered him to his mother.

And there came a fear on all: and they glorified God, saying, That a great prophet is risen up among us; and, That God hath visited his people.

—*Luke 7:11–16*

— Ten —

Living the Life of Praise

How easy it is for our vision to become narrowly focused, brought down to only what is immediately in front of us: the next problem to solve, the next project to begin. The Scriptures lift our vision to more worthy sights. And as we contemplate the unending expanse of this universe, the breadth of His Creation, and the depth of His love, we can only respond with heartfelt thanks and praise.

181

Seek Your Fulfillment in God Alone

O God, from whom to be turned is to fall;
To whom to be turned is to rise;
From whom to depart is to die;
To whom to return is to revive;
In whom to dwell is to live
Whom no man loses unless he be deceived,
Whom no man seeks unless has has been
admonished,
Whom no man finds unless he has been
purified.
Whom to abandon is to perish,
To reach out to whom is to love,
To see whom is true possession.

— *Augustine of Hippo* [1]

Whoso trusteth in the LORD, happy is he.
—*Proverbs 16:20b*

Acquaint now thyself with him, and be at peace: thereby good shall come unto thee.

Receive, I pray thee, the law from his mouth, and lay up his words in thine heart.

182

If thou return to the Almighty, thou shalt be built up, thou shalt put away iniquity far from thy tabernacles.

Then shalt thou lay up gold as dust, and the gold of Ophir as the stones of the brooks.

Yea, the Almighty shall be thy defence, and thou shalt have plenty of silver.

For then shalt thou have thy delight in the Almighty, and shalt lift up thy face unto God.

—*Job 22:21–26*

Happy art thou, O Israel: who is like unto thee, O people saved by the LORD, the shield of thy help, and who is the sword of thy excellency! and thine enemies shall be found liars unto thee; and thou shalt tread upon their high places.

—*Deuteronomy 33:29*

They shall be abundantly satisfied with the fatness of thy house; and thou shalt make them drink of the river of thy pleasures.

—*Psalm 36:8*

I delight to do thy will, O my God: yea, thy law is within my heart.

—Psalm 40:8

My soul shall be satisfied as with marrow and fatness; and my mouth shall praise thee with joyful lips.

—Psalm 63:5

Blessed is every one that feareth the LORD; that walketh in his ways.

For thou shalt eat the labour of thine hands: happy shalt thou be, and it shall be well with thee.

—Psalm 128:1–2

Happy is that people, that is in such a case: yea, happy is that people, whose God is the LORD.

—Psalm 144:15

Happy is he that hath the God of Jacob for his help, whose hope is in the LORD his God.

—Psalm 146:5

He that despiseth his neighbour sinneth: but he that hath mercy on the poor, happy is he.

—*Proverbs 14:21*

Cultivate a Spirit of Gratitude

Gratitude is born in hearts that take time to count up past mercies.

—*Charles Jefferson*

In every thing give thanks: for this is the will of God in Christ Jesus concerning you.

—*1 Thessalonians 5:18*

[King Solomon] turned his face about, and blessed all the congregation of Israel: (and all the congregation of Israel stood;)

And he said, Blessed be the LORD God of Israel, which spake with his mouth unto David my father, and hath with his hand fulfilled it, saying,

Since the day that I brought forth my people Israel out of Egypt, I chose no city out of all the tribes of Israel to build an house, that my name might be therein; but I chose David to be over my people Israel.

And it was in the heart of David my father to build an house for the name of the LORD God of Israel.

And the LORD said unto David my father, Whereas it was in thine heart to build an house unto my name, thou didst well that it was in thine heart.

Nevertheless thou shalt not build the house; but thy son that shall come forth out of thy loins, he shall build the house unto my name.

And the LORD hath performed his word that he spake, and I am risen up in the room of David my father, and sit on the throne of Israel, as the LORD promised, and have built an house for the name of the LORD God of Israel.

And I have set there a place for the ark, wherein is the covenant of the LORD, which he made with our fathers, when he brought them out of the land of Egypt.

—*1 Kings 8:14–21*

Be careful for nothing; but in every thing by prayer and supplication with thanksgiving let your requests be made known unto God.

—*Philippians 4:6*

Enjoy the Life He Has Given You

That gift of his, from God descended.
Ah! friend, what gift of man's does not?

—*Robert Browning*

The LORD is the portion of mine inheritance and of my cup: thou maintainest my lot.

The lines are fallen unto me in pleasant places; yea, I have a goodly heritage.

—*Psalm 16:5–6*

Thou hast turned for me my mourning into dancing: thou hast put off my sackcloth, and girded me with gladness;

To the end that my glory may sing praise to thee, and not be silent. O LORD my God, I will give thanks unto thee for ever.

—*Psalm 30:11–12*

He maketh the barren woman to keep house, and to be a joyful mother of children. Praise ye the LORD.

—*Psalm 113:9*

They that sow in tears shall reap in joy. He that goeth forth and weepeth, bearing precious seed, shall doubtless come again with rejoicing, bringing his sheaves with him.

—*Psalm 126:5–6*

Sing, O ye heavens; for the LORD hath done it: shout, ye lower parts of the earth: break forth into singing, ye mountains, O forest, and every tree therein: for the LORD hath redeemed Jacob, and glorified himself in Israel.

—*Isaiah 44:23*

Thou hast loved righteousness, and hated iniquity; therefore God, even thy God, hath anointed thee with the oil of gladness above thy fellows.

—*Hebrews 1:9*

My brethren, count it all joy when ye fall into divers temptations;

Knowing this, that the trying of your faith worketh patience.

But let patience have her perfect work, that ye may be perfect and entire, wanting nothing.

If any of you lack wisdom, let him ask of God, that giveth to all men liberally, and upbraideth not; and it shall be given him.

But let him ask in faith, nothing wavering. For he that wavereth is like a wave of the sea driven with the wind and tossed.

—*James 1:2–6*

But rejoice, inasmuch as ye are partakers of Christ's sufferings; that, when his glory shall be revealed, ye may be glad also with exceeding joy.

—*1 Peter 4:13*

189

Offer Praise and Thanks Every Day

God, I give You the praise for days well spent. But I am yet unsatisfied, because I do not enjoy enough of You. I apprehend myself at too great a distance from You. I would have my soul more closely united to You by faith and love.

—*Susanna Wesley*

O come, let us worship and bow down: let us kneel before the LORD our maker.

—*Psalm 95:6*

Then was the secret revealed unto Daniel in a night vision. Then Daniel blessed the God of heaven.

Daniel answered and said, Blessed be the name of God for ever and ever: for wisdom and might are his:

And he changeth the times and the seasons: he removeth kings, and setteth up kings: he giveth wisdom unto the wise, and knowledge to them that know understanding:

He revealeth the deep and secret things: he knoweth what is in the darkness, and the light dwelleth with him.

I thank thee, and praise thee, O thou God of my fathers, who hast given me wisdom and might, and hast made known unto me now what we desired of thee: for thou hast now made known unto us the king's matter.

—*Daniel 2:19–23*

Be careful for nothing; but in every thing by prayer and supplication with thanksgiving let your requests be made known unto God.

—*Philippians 4:6*

The heavens declare the glory of God; and the firmament sheweth his handywork.

Day unto day uttereth speech, and night unto night sheweth knowledge.

There is no speech nor language, where their voice is not heard.

Their line is gone out through all the earth, and their words to the end of the world. In them hath he set a tabernacle for the sun.

—*Psalm 19:1–4*

191

I will sing of the mercies of the LORD for ever: with my mouth will I make known thy faithfulness to all generations.

For I have said, Mercy shall be built up for ever: thy faithfulness shalt thou establish in the very heavens.

I have made a covenant with my chosen, I have sworn unto David my servant,

Thy seed will I establish for ever, and build up thy throne to all generations. Selah.

—*Psalm 89:1–4*

The LORD shall increase you more and more, you and your children.

Ye are blessed of the LORD which made heaven and earth.

The heaven, even the heavens, are the LORD's: but the earth hath he given to the children of men.

The dead praise not the LORD, neither any that go down into silence.

But we will bless the LORD from this time forth and for evermore. Praise the LORD.

—*Psalm 115:14–18*

This is the day which the LORD hath made; we will rejoice and be glad in it.

—Psalm 118:24

I will extol thee, my God, O king; and I will bless thy name for ever and ever.

Every day will I bless thee; and I will praise thy name for ever and ever.

Great is the LORD, and greatly to be praised; and his greatness is unsearchable.

One generation shall praise thy works to another, and shall declare thy mighty acts.

—Psalm 145:1–4

Praise ye the LORD. Praise God in his sanctuary: praise him in the firmament of his power.

Praise him for his mighty acts: praise him according to his excellent greatness.

Praise him with the sound of the trumpet: praise him with the psaltery and harp.

Praise him with the timbrel and dance: praise him with stringed instruments and organs.

Praise him upon the loud cymbals: praise him upon the high sounding cymbals.

Let every thing that hath breath praise the LORD. Praise ye the LORD.

—Psalm 150

Then saith Jesus unto him, Get thee hence, Satan: for it is written, Thou shalt worship the Lord thy God, and him only shalt thou serve.

—*Matthew 4:10*

Jesus saith unto her, Woman, believe me, the hour cometh, when ye shall neither in this mountain, nor yet at Jerusalem, worship the Father.

Ye worship ye know not what: we know what we worship: for salvation is of the Jews.

But the hour cometh, and now is, when the true worshippers shall worship the Father in spirit and in truth: for the Father seeketh such to worship him.

God is a Spirit: and they that worship him must worship him in spirit and in truth.

—*John 4:21–24*

Let the word of Christ dwell in you richly in all wisdom; teaching and admonishing one another in psalms and hymns and spiritual songs, singing with grace in your hearts to the Lord.

—*Colossians 3:16*

In every thing give thanks: for this is the will of God in Christ Jesus concerning you.
—*1 Thessalonians 5:18*

Echo the Psalmist's Worship in Your Own Life!

For worship is a thirsty land crying out for rain,
It is a candle in the act of being kindled,
It is a drop in quest of the ocean . . .
It is a voice in the night calling for help,
It is a soul standing in awe before the mystery of the universe . . .
It is time flowing into eternity . . .
a man climbing the altar stairs to God.

—*Dwight Bradley* [2]

I will praise thee with my whole heart: before the gods will I sing praise unto thee.

I will worship toward thy holy temple, and praise thy name for thy lovingkindness and for thy truth: for thou hast magnified thy word above all thy name.

195

In the day when I cried thou answeredst me, and strengthenedst me with strength in my soul.

All the kings of the earth shall praise thee, O LORD, when they hear the words of thy mouth.

Yea, they shall sing in the ways of the LORD: for great is the glory of the LORD.

Though the LORD be high, yet hath he respect unto the lowly: but the proud he knoweth afar off.

Though I walk in the midst of trouble, thou wilt revive me: thou shalt stretch forth thine hand against the wrath of mine enemies, and thy right hand shall save me.

The LORD will perfect that which concerneth me: thy mercy, O LORD, endureth for ever: forsake not the works of thine own hands.

—*Psalm 138*

I will speak of the glorious honour of thy majesty, and of thy wondrous works.

And men shall speak of the might of thy terrible acts: and I will declare thy greatness.

They shall abundantly utter the memory of thy great goodness, and shall sing of thy righteousness.

The LORD is gracious, and full of compassion; slow to anger, and of great mercy.

The LORD is good to all: and his tender mercies are over all his works.

All thy works shall praise thee, O LORD; and thy saints shall bless thee.

They shall speak of the glory of thy kingdom, and talk of thy power;

To make known to the sons of men his mighty acts, and the glorious majesty of his kingdom.

Thy kingdom is an everlasting kingdom, and thy dominion endureth throughout all generations.

The LORD upholdeth all that fall, and raiseth up all those that be bowed down.

The eyes of all wait upon thee; and thou givest them their meat in due season.

Thou openest thine hand, and satisfiest the desire of every living thing.

The LORD is righteous in all his ways, and holy in all his works.

The LORD is nigh unto all them that call upon him, to all that call upon him in truth.

He will fulfil the desire of them that fear him: he also will hear their cry, and will save them.

The LORD preserveth all them that love him: but all the wicked will he destroy.

My mouth shall speak the praise of the LORD: and let all flesh bless his holy name for ever and ever.

—*Psalm 145:5–21*

Notes

—Chapter One—

1 Donald T. Kauffman, *Gist of the Lesson.*
2 James Hewett, in *Illustrations Unlimited* (Wheaton, Ill.: Tyndale, 1988).
3 Ibid.

—Chapter Two—

1 John Powell, in *The Secret of Staying in Love.*
2 Peter Ustinov, quoted in "Points to Ponder," *Reader's Digest*, October 1992.
3 Leslie D. Weatherhead, in *The Complete Book of Christian Prayer* (New York: Continuum, 1995).
4 David V. Andersen, in *Christianity Today*, 19 July 1993.

—Chapter Three—

1 Sir James George Frazer, in *The Golden Bough*, published in 1922.

—Chapter Four—

1 Dietrich Bonhoeffer, in *The Cost of Discipleship* (New York: Macmillan, 1961).
2 James Dobson, in *Ministries Today*, December 1995.

—Chapter Five—

1 James Hewett, in *Illustrations Unlimited* (Wheaton, Ill.: Tyndale, 1988).

2 Hugh Blackburne, in *The Complete Book of Christian Prayer* (New York: Continuum, 1995).

—Chapter Six—

1 David Augsburger, *Caring Enough to Confront* (Glendale, Calif: Regal Books, 1976).

—Chapter Seven—

1 Doug Sherman and William Hendricks, *Your Work Matters to God* (Colorado Springs: Navpress, 1993).

—Chapter Ten—

1 Augustine of Hippo, Soliloquies, 1.3, quoted in Michael Marshall, *The Restless Heart* (Grand Rapids: William B. Eerdmans, 1987), 74.
2 Dwight Bradley, in *Leaves from a Spiritual Notebook,* as quoted in Frank S. Mead, ed., *12,000 Religious Quotations* (Grand Rapids: Baker, 1992).